SCHLOSS III

✳ ✳ ✳

THE FASCINATING ROYAL HISTORY OF 25 CASTLES IN CENTRAL GERMANY

SUSAN SYMONS

Published by Roseland Books
The Old Rectory, St Just-in-Roseland, Truro, Cornwall, TR2 5JD

ISBN 13: 978-0-9928014-4-1
ISBN 10: 0992801443

For my dear grandson, Samuel, who I hope will enjoy history.

CONTENTS

1. Introduction   1

2. North Rhine-Westphalia, the Wittelsbach family,
   and the House of Lippe.   9
   Augustusburg   10
   Nordkirchen   20
   Bensberg   24
   Burg Vischering   30
   Burg Altena   33
   Detmold   38

3. Lower Saxony and the princes of Waldeck-Pyrmont   47
   Pyrmont   48
   Bevern   56

4. Saxony-Anhalt and the Anhalt family   61
   Johannbau   62
   Mosigkau   67
   Wörlitz Country House   71
   Quedlinburg Abbey Castle   77

5. Thuringia and the dukes of Saxe-Meiningen   85
   The Wartburg   86
   Elisabethenburg   94
   Altenstein   100
   Wilhelmsburg   106

6. **Hesse and the House of Hesse**   113
    Grand Ducal Schloss, Darmstadt   114
    Jagdschloss Kranichstein   121
    Heiligenberg   126
    Burg Friedberg   134
    Wilhelmshöhe   138
    Wilhelmsthal   144

7. **Rhineland-Palatinate, the Nassau-Diez and**   149
    Hohenzollern families
    Bathhouse Palace, Bad Ems   150
    Oranienstein   157
    Stolzenfels   163

8. **Reflections**   173

Appendices   179
    A. Map of Germany   180
    B. List of the schlösser included in my books   182
    C. List of Germany's royal families   186
    D. Charts and family trees   187

Illustration Credits   203

Notes   204

Bibliography   213

The *Schloss* series of books   217

1

INTRODUCTION

Almost a hundred years ago, at the end of World War I, the Kaiser abdicated and Germany became a republic. This was the end of a thousand years of German monarchy. From the crowning of Otto I in 962, to the abdication of Wilhelm II in 1918, Germany was a patchwork of royal states, held together under the banner of an empire. The dukes and princes who ruled these states were passionate builders and often led tumultuous lives. It is their beautiful castles and palaces, and their colourful personal stories, which provide the material for my books.

Schloss is the German word for castle or palace and I started to write about these after my husband and I began to spend time in Germany each spring. This book includes twenty-five different *schlösser* (that's the plural of schloss) in the central part of Germany and looks at these from two different aspects. One is my experience as an overseas visitor at each schloss, as part of researching the book; the other, some of the colourful historical stories about the royal characters associated with them. Royalty have always been the celebrities of their day, and these stories from history can rival anything in modern-day television soap operas. The royal stories in this book include the prince who defied his family to marry a pharmacist's daughter and then purchased the rank of royal princess for her; the discarded mistress whose severance package from the king included the deputy headship of a finishing school for princesses; the prince cheated out of his inheritance by his elder brothers after their father's will disappeared; and the princess whose illegitimate birth may have been covered-up and who married the heir to the Russian throne.

The definition of 'schloss'

A narrow translation of the word **schloss** into English is castle but the word is used more widely in German and can denote any type of grand residence – ranging from a fortified castle (also called a burg), to a stately royal palace (palais), to a manor house (herrenhaus).

A prefix can also be added to give more information about the schloss. So – a **residenzschloss** was the main residence and seat of government of a ruling prince and would be in the capital of his state; in contrast a **jagdschloss** was a hunting lodge and would be in a more remote location in the forest or countryside. The prefix can also say something about how the building was constructed – a **hangburg** was built on a hillside, and a **wasserschloss** in the waters of a lake.

Schloss III takes the reader on a circular tour through six of Germany's federal states in the central part of the country, starting and ending at the river Rhine. The six states are (in the order of the book) – North Rhine-Westphalia, Lower Saxony, Saxony-Anhalt, Thuringia, Hesse, and Rhineland-Palatinate. The book is laid out with a chapter for each state and within that a section for each schloss. Appendix A at the back of the book has a map of Germany showing the federal states and the approximate location of each of the twenty-five schlösser. Two of the states – Saxony-Anhalt and Thuringia – were in East Germany during the years after World War II when Germany was divided into two countries. But, even more than twenty-five years after reunification, much of this part of Germany is still not well known to foreign tourists.

I hope my *Schloss* books might encourage more overseas visitors to go to German schlösser, particularly visitors from the UK and USA. Whilst a few, such as Frederick the Great's Sanssouci in Brandenburg (included in my first book) are on the tourist trail, there are so many more that rarely see an English-speaking visitor. What my husband and I call *Schloss Hunting* has taken us to some stunningly beautiful parts of Germany, to see schlösser with riveting historical stories. It has also given us some adventures. When researching for this book, we bumped into a television crew at Altenstein (chapter five) and appeared in their TV programme about schlösser; were escorted across an army base to see Oranienstein (chapter seven); and had the new Battenberg family museum in Heiligenberg (chapter six) opened up especially for us!

One reason for writing my books is to share my view that history need not be dry-as-dust, and that the history of royalty in particular is fascinating and fun. The stories of royal lives can tell us a lot about the times in which they lived and Germany was right at the centre of the system of European monarchy. The patchwork of little German states was the cradle of kings, and when the duke of Hannover became King George I of Great Britain in 1714 (after the death of his distant cousin Queen Anne), it was just one example of a German prince taking over the throne of another European country. Arranged marriages protected the bloodlines of Europe's royalty, and Germany was also the royal marriage market because of its plentiful supply of eligible princesses. German princesses were chosen to be empresses and queens and to fulfil the greatest roles in the society of their day. Every monarch of Britain from George I to Queen Victoria married a German princess or, in the case of Victoria, a German prince.

At the back of this book are two appendices which I hope will assist in getting to grips with the tight network of royal families. Appendix C gives a list of Germany's ruling families in 1815, after the political reorganisation at the end of the Napoleonic Wars; and appendix D includes charts and family trees to illustrate some of the royal stories – they are referred to at appropriate points in the text.

The History of Germany

It may be helpful for the reader to have a broad outline of the political history of Germany as background for the stories in this book. The key point to bear in mind is that Germany was not a single nation-state but a federation of numerous independent territories, each with its own ruler and royal family. This was the case right up until the end of World War I, when the monarchy came to an end and Germany became a republic.

For nearly a thousand years the independent German states were held together as part of the **Holy Roman Empire**, under an elected emperor. The start of the empire is usually dated as 962, when Otto I was crowned; the end came in 1806 when Francis II disbanded the empire after it became unstable during the Napoleonic Wars. Over the next century there were several successive groupings of the royal states – first the **Confederation of the Rhine** led by Napoleon; then, from 1815, the **German Confederation** under Austrian presidency; and finally, from 1871, the **German Empire** with a Prussian kaiser (emperor).

At the end of World War I revolution swept across Germany and Kaiser Wilhelm II abdicated, followed swiftly by all the other royal rulers. A republic was declared and an armistice to end the war signed on 11 November 1918. The new **Weimar Republic** was a parliamentary democracy, but was politically unstable from the start – tainted by the punitive peace terms and plagued by economic problems. In 1933 it was supplanted by a **Nazi dictatorship** under Hitler, who led Germany into World War II.

After the war Germany was divided into zones of occupation and this hardened in 1949 when Germany became two separate countries – the Federal Republic of Germany (known as **West Germany**) and the German Democratic Republic (known as **East Germany** or **the GDR**). West Germany comprised the American, British, and French zones and was a parliamentary democracy with a capitalist economy. The GDR (previously the Soviet zone) was communist and part of the Soviet bloc. The two countries were separated by an Iron Curtain until the fall of communism and the **Reunification of Germany** in 1990.

I have now been fortunate to visit more than a hundred schlösser in the course of researching my books. Appendix B provides a complete list of these, showing their location and the royal family associated with them. From these visits, I have really come to appreciate the durability of these wonderful buildings and how they have adapted across the centuries to meet the changing times. The last chapter of this book (called Reflections) explores how these large buildings have survived the one hundred years since the monarchy fell, and how they are being used today.

The contents of this book are a blend of historical information and my own observations and impressions about each of the schlösser included. My comments are from the perspective of an overseas visitor who does not speak German, and come from my experience of visiting each particular schloss on a particular day. I must stress that they are entirely personal; another visitor on a different day could have an entirely different experience. The sources I have consulted for the historical information are shown in the notes section and the bibliography at the back of the book. Please note this book is not a detailed travel guide and readers will need to consult the schlösser websites, or other information, for opening hours and directions. The book is illustrated throughout with a mixture of present-day photographs, old postcards, and royal portraits.

This is my third book about the fascinating royal history of German schlösser. Details of the first two, called *Schloss* and *Schloss II* are shown at the back of this book. I hope all three books might appeal to anyone who likes history or travelogues or who is interested in people's personal stories. I have had a huge amount of fun visiting the schlösser and writing these three books, and am already planning a fourth – with twenty-five schlösser in south Germany and the state of Bavaria!

While researching my books I have been constantly surprised at the tight links which bound Europe's royalty together, including the close connections between the German and the British royal families. In 2005 Prince Philip (the husband of Queen Elizabeth II) made a visit to the village of Jugenheim, a few miles south of Darmstadt in Hesse. With him was the youngest of his three sons, Prince Edward. This was not an official visit; they came privately to see a country house which, before Prince Philip's grandfather sold it in 1920, belonged to his family. Today Schloss Heiligenberg is a business centre and events venue, but the connections with Prince Philip's family are still treasured. The museum at the schloss has memories of the golden days when royalty from all over Europe gathered here in summer, before World War I brought this world crashing to an end. (See chapter six for more on Heiligenberg.)

Different architectural styles

Over the centuries architectural styles changed, as building techniques developed and the use of schlösser evolved. This note provides a brief outline of what characterises the different architectural styles referred to in this book. The dates mentioned are very approximate and indicative only, as in reality dates and styles merged and overlapped.

The earliest schlösser were fortified castles, built as strongholds against attack. Around 1200 AD, the **Romanesque** *style of architecture (named after the Roman Empire), which was characterised by round arches, thick walls, and small windows, gave way to the* **Gothic** *style (named after the Visigoths, who sacked Rome), when improvements in building techniques enabled taller structures, pointed arches and larger windows. The Palas building of the Wartburg in chapter five dates from the twelfth century and is in romanesque style; the oldest parts of Burg Friedberg in chapter six are examples of gothic architecture.*

From around 1500, schlösser began to evolve from defensive castles into palaces, designed to house a ruler's court and to show off his wealth and power. **Renaissance** *architecture (meaning rebirth) harked back to classical Greece and Rome, and is characterised by symmetry, proportion, and ornamented gables. Schloss Bevern in chapter three was built in the early 1600s in renaissance style.*

During the 1600s the more elaborate **Baroque** style came into fashion, characterised by lavish decoration, complicated shapes, and grand staircases. (The name baroque is from the Portuguese word for a natural pearl.) Baroque schlösser, such as Augustusburg in chapter two built in the first half of the 1700s, are intended to impress and dazzle the eye. They are a physical manifestation of the idea of the divine right of princes to rule, and a symbol of absolute power. During the second half of the 1700s, baroque architecture developed a lighter, frothier, touch called **Rococo** (after the French for shell). Schloss Wilhelmsthal in chapter six is an example of this delicate style, which uses curves, light colours, and naturalistic themes.

From the late 1700s, **Classical** architecture was a reaction against ornate decoration and a return to the ideas of ancient Greece and Rome. Schlösser in this style are austere and grand, with huge columns, pediments and domes. Schloss Wilhelmshöhe in chapter six, built in the last years of the eighteenth century, is an example of the classical style.

During the 1800s schlösser were built or remodelled in **Historicist** style, which imitated the architecture of the past. For example Stolzenfels, a ruined castle on the river Rhine in chapter seven, was rebuilt between 1835 and 1842 in **Neo (or mock)-gothic** style, as a romantic and imagined version of a medieval castle. And at the end of the nineteenth century Altenstein, in chapter five, was also transformed – from eighteenth century baroque into a **Neo-renaissance** version of an English country house.

2

NORTH RHINE-WESTPHALIA, THE WITTELSBACH FAMILY, AND THE HOUSE OF LIPPE

We start in the federal state of North Rhine-Westphalia in the west of the country, bordering the Netherlands and Belgium. The state includes two quite different and distinct historic areas, both centred on a river. One is the beautiful Rhineland along the River Rhine, which runs from south to north through the western part of the state. Called *Father Rhine* (Vater Rhein), this river has a special place in the hearts and minds of Germans. The other area is Westphalia, the industrial powerhouse of Germany, which is to the east of the Rhine, and through the centre of which flows the River Ruhr from east to west, to join the Rhine at Duisburg.

In the days of the Holy Roman Empire, before the French emperor Napoleon changed the political structure of Germany for ever, North Rhine-Westphalia was made up of numerous small states. We saw schlösser from several of these and discovered some gripping stories, including a disputed inheritance involving a secret contract, concealed death, and a sensational court case. Our first schloss is in what was, until French troops invaded in 1794, a state called the electorate of Cologne. It was built by a great prince with a mania for building, and it's where Queen Victoria spent her very first night in Germany.

Augustusburg

At Brühl, on the left bank of the Rhine between Cologne and Bonn, we visited the magnificent baroque summer palace created by Clemens August, archbishop-elector of Cologne. He was one of the most powerful princes in Germany who held numerous high offices and was the brother of the Holy Roman emperor. Clemens August was a passionate builder and there are other beautiful schlösser that are part of his building legacy. But the most impressive are the two he built at Brühl – Schloss Augustusburg (August's castle) and its satellite Jagdschloss (or hunting lodge) Falkenlust (Falcons' Delight). These and the gardens that surround them are so important historically and architecturally that they are a UNESCO World Heritage Site.

1. Schloss Augustusburg; the magnificent baroque summer palace built by Clemens August, archbishop-elector of Cologne.

Our first sight of Augustusburg was from the railway station at Brühl, where we parked the car. This might sound incongruous but actually it was quite appropriate; the railway was built close to the schloss and from the early days of rail guests arrived this way. The first state visitor to travel here by the new railway was Queen Victoria when she came to stay at Augustusburg with her husband, Prince Albert, in August 1845[1]. There were crowds to see the royal couple arrive at the station, with their host King Friedrich Wilhelm IV of Prussia. Victoria travelled the short distance to the schloss by carriage and horses, but we walked from the station, down a wide cobbled path laid out in squares like a chequer board. The schloss is horse-shoe shaped, with a shorter central wing and two longer side wings that protrude forwards. It felt as if these side wings were drawing us in.

It was the first day of Queen Victoria's first visit to Germany and she was very excited to be in her husband's home country. Prince Albert was a prince of Saxe-Coburg-Gotha and had attended the University of Bonn before his marriage. On the evening of her arrival there was a military tattoo in the *Cour D'Honneur* (the open courtyard in front of the schloss), lit by torches and coloured lanterns. Five hundred military musicians took part and the highlight was the *Great Tattoo* – a finale of two hundred drummers drumming. The royal guests watched from the first floor windows and a crowd of twenty thousand from outside the schloss gates. Victoria wrote in her journal that it was the finest thing she had ever seen or heard[2]. It was amazing to think that such pageantry had taken place where we were standing.

Clemens August laid the foundation stone for Augustusburg in 1725, while he was a young man. But there were three different architects and several changes of plan, and building work was not completed when he died unexpectedly in 1761. This building was always designed to impress and to show off the rank and power of the prince who built it. The facade is decorated and painted in yellow, white, and grey. On the grand pediment of the main wing are the symbols and badges of Clemens August's high birth and the great positions he held.

11

Clemens August was a Wittelsbach prince from the old Bavarian line. The Wittelsbach family had separate branches who ruled Bavaria in southern Germany and the Palatine (another German state) on the middle Rhine. Born in 1700, Clemens August was the fourth son of Maximilian II Emanuel, the elector (or sovereign) of Bavaria. He had a fractured childhood; his father was exiled from Bavaria (for taking sides against the Holy Roman emperor) and the family were split up for over ten years[3]. Maximilian II Emanuel had five surviving sons and, when the family were reunited, he decided only two should marry and have children to carry on the family line; the other three, including Clemens August, would enter the church[4]. Time would show that this was not a great decision, as his line of the Wittelsbach family died out with Maximilian II Emanuel's grandson.

2. This portrait of Clemens August shows the badges of his high office – the elector's crown, the cross of the Teutonic Order, and his bishop's mitre.

At sixteen, in accordance with his father's decision, Clemens August and his older brother Philippe Moritz (also designated by their father for the church) went to Rome to study under the personal supervision of the pope. They were still in Italy three years later when fate took a hand and, in 1719, Philippe Moritz died. Before this became known in Germany however, Philippe Moritz was appointed prince-bishop both of Paderborn and of Münster in Westphalia. These were important positions – a prince-bishop was the spiritual head of a religious diocese, and also the sovereign ruler of an independent state in the Holy Roman Empire. It was desired to keep them in the Wittelsbach family and after some lobbying they were transferred to Clemens August. His spectacular career as a church prince had begun!

More positions followed and soon Clemens August held five prince-bishoprics, earning him the nickname of *Monsieur de Cinq-Églises* or prince of five churches[5]. He became archbishop-elector of Cologne in 1723, prince-bishop of Hildesheim in 1724, and prince-bishop of Osnabrück in 1728. No matter that the rules of the church forbade the holding of more than one office simultaneously – the pope just conveniently obliged with a dispensation each time, making the condition only that Clemens August be ordained, which he was in 1725. A final title was added in 1732 when Clemens August also became Grand Master of the Teutonic Order. This carried no territory or ruling rights; it did however come with significant revenues which he used to fund his building programme. The most important of Clemens August's titles was that of archbishop-elector of Cologne, because it gave him the prestigious position of an elector of the Holy Roman Empire.

So Clemens August became one of the most important princes in Germany. In the portrait in this book he is shown with badges of his high office – the elector's cap or crown, the cross of the Teutonic Order, and his bishop's mitre. In the background is his beloved hunting lodge, called Falkenlust (see later in this section). The high point in his career came when he crowned his eldest brother as the Holy Roman Emperor Karl VII in Frankfurt cathedral in 1742.

But Karl VII did not prove a very successful or long-lived emperor. He had stood for election against an Austrian candidate and even while he was being crowned, his home country of Bavaria was overrun by Austrian troops. He died in 1745, shortly after Bavaria was restored to him. Karl was succeeded as elector of Bavaria by his only son, Maximilian III Joseph. He had no children, so that when Maximilian III Joseph died in 1777 this branch of the Wittelsbach family came to an end. Their distant relatives from the Palatine branch of the family then also became rulers of Bavaria. Chart 1 in appendix D is a family tree for the Bavarian branch of the Wittelsbach family.

Entrance to Augustusburg is by guided tour, with a foreign language audiotape for overseas visitors. We arrived just after the first tour had left but, as there was only one visitor on this, the museum attendants hurried us through the first rooms to join it. So, almost before we knew it, we were standing in the masterpiece of the schloss – the Treppenhaus or ceremonial staircase. This is one of the most astonishingly beautiful spaces I have seen. It is also something of a conjuring trick.

3. The beautiful ceremonial staircase at Augustusburg, seen from the ground floor; when you climb the first flight of stairs, a glorious vista opens up.

The Wittelsbach electors of Cologne

The electorate of Cologne was a sovereign territory in the Holy Roman Empire ruled by the archbishop of Cologne. Despite its name the electorate did not include the city of Cologne itself, which was a self-governing city within the empire. The capital of the electorate was in Bonn.

The electorate was one of the most important states in the empire because it carried the position of elector. In the time of Clemens August there were only nine of these – three archbishop-electors, of Cologne, Mainz and Trier; and six prince-electors, (or kurfürsten) – the rulers of Bavaria, Bohemia, Brandenburg, Hannover, the Palatine and Saxony. The nine were responsible for electing the emperor and were the highest-ranking princes in the empire, second in status only to the emperor himself.

The position of archbishop-elector of Cologne was not hereditary (unlike the ruler of a secular state) but was held continuously by the same family for one hundred and eighty years. Between 1583 and 1761 five successive princes from the Bavarian branch of the Wittelsbach family were appointed archbishop-elector (see chart 1). Clemens August was the last of the five.

The electorate of Cologne was abolished in 1803, along with most of the other church states, as part of a massive shake-up of the structure of the Holy Roman Empire driven by Napoleon. Their lands were distributed among the secular states. The electorate had already been truncated when its lands on the left bank of the Rhine were occupied by France in 1794 and later annexed. The Holy Roman Empire itself was dissolved in 1806. After the eventual defeat of Napoleon in 1815 at the battle of Waterloo, most of what had been the electorate of Cologne became part of Prussia.

Standing with the guide on the ground floor at the bottom of the staircase, I was overwhelmed by the glowing colours, the gorgeous pillars and statues, and the superb metal railings. But it was not until we climbed the first flight of stairs that the whole vista opened up. The staircase rises gloriously through four floors of amazing and elaborate decoration to a ceiling painting twenty metres above, the colours becoming lighter as it goes. The theme of all this magnificent decoration is, of course, Clemens August himself – his high birth and rank, his glory, and his power as an absolute ruler. A gilded bust of the archbishop-elector looks down upon it all. The staircase was cleverly designed to make the best use of the limited space, and to draw the eye up. The effect is stupendous and uplifting. I read in one book that the staircase at Augustusburg could 'make a choir burst spontaneously into song'[6].

The Treppenhaus was built in the 1740s to replace an original staircase that Clemens August did not consider to be grand enough for the ceremonial reception of visitors. The etiquette at his court decreed that, depending on their rank, visitors should be officially received at up to four different places before entering his audience chamber[7]. The new staircase was designed by a famous architect called Balthasar Neumann, who had a reputation for staircases and had created other celebrated examples (including in the Hofburg in Vienna) before Clemens August brought him in at Augustusburg.

4. The Summer Dining Hall at Augustusburg was designed to stay cool in hot weather, with tiled walls and a marble floor.

After the Treppenhaus, I was concerned that the rest of the tour could be an anti-climax, but I need not have worried – we went through one gorgeous room after another along the suite of state apartments – the Hall of the Guards, the Dining and Music Room, Audience Hall, and State Bedchamber, to name just some of these. The state apartments are on the first floor, and beneath them on the ground floor are a suite of rooms with a similar layout called the summer apartments, which open directly on the gardens. I liked the Summer Dining Hall, designed to stay cool in hot weather. The walls are covered in blue and white tiles (the Wittelsbach colours) and the floor is marble. I could feel my feet getting cold! In the middle of the room hangs a wonderful chandelier of white Murano glass, made to look like ice.

Clemens August's greatest love after his building projects, and the next biggest cost to his treasury, was hunting with falcons. He was mad about falcons and at Augustusburg even his privy (lavatory) is decorated with paintings of these! Hunting was more than a leisure pursuit for princes of his day; it was considered that only those who demonstrated the virtues required for hunting – discipline, perseverance and farsightedness – were fit to hold high offices of state[8]. Clemens August was attracted to Brühl for his summer residence because this area was good for breeding the herons which were his falcons' prey.

In the gardens of Augustusburg, Clemens August built a small and exquisite hunting lodge called Falkenlust, or Falcons' Delight. This was a private place where he could retreat with boon companions to pursue his chosen pastimes. He used it not only for falconry but also for his love life. Falkenlust was where his lady friends were invited to a rendezvous. He even lent it to Casanova to entertain the wife of the mayor of Cologne, when Casanova was trying to seduce her[9]. Although holding a high position in the church, Clemens August still lived the lifestyle of a prince of his time and is known to have had love affairs. He acknowledged his illegitimate daughter, Ann Marie, by a beautiful harpist called Mechthild Brion, and later arranged for this daughter to marry the illegitimate son of his oldest brother Karl, (who was briefly Holy Roman emperor)[10].

17

5. In the gardens of Augustusburg Clemens August built
an exquisite hunting lodge called Falkenlust.

If you have not been there, I urge you to go and see Augustusburg for yourself. When Napoleon visited in 1804 he liked the schloss so much that he wished it had wheels and he could take it back to France[11]. The schloss is very welcoming to foreign visitors – the attendants spoke English, there is an English guidebook, and a very lively English audio guide which is full of interesting information and stories. I heard, for example, about the personal hygiene regime of Clemens August – he rarely took a bath, but sponged himself daily with Eau de Cologne (a scent named after his electorate). The records show he ordered up to forty flasks of this a month, or one a day! It would not have rid him of the lice and fleas which were a daily fact of life in the eighteenth century and the audio guide also explained the mechanics of a flea trap. There was a model of one of these in the plasterwork on the ceiling of the Cabinet, where Clemens August carried out his personal grooming. It was a small container full of holes, worn in a wig or crinoline. The fleas were attracted to a blood-soaked cloth inside the trap, where they would get stuck on some adhesive.

The problems of today's world – Schloss Türnich

After we left Augustusburg my husband and I decided to drive around and explore the locality, and that's how we found Schloss Türnich at Kerpen. We had a delicious lunch in the Schloss Café, which serves organic, vegetarian food. By chance we also bumped into the son of the owner, who told us about the history of the schloss and its present predicament.

Türnich has a connection with Clemens August, archbishop-elector of Cologne. As well as his own building projects, Clemens August encouraged other noble families to use his architects and craftsmen and build their schlösser in the area. Türnich was probably the work of Michael Leveilly, the master builder at Clemens August's court who supervised the building work at Augustusburg[12]. In 1850 Türnich was bought by the Grafs von und zu Hoensbroech, who originated in Holland, and they still own it today.

The predicament at Türnich is a dramatic fall in the level of the water table, caused by the impact of nearby massive-scale opencast mining. The schloss has been undermined and is unstable and uninhabitable. The problem affects the whole area; we were told that other schlösser have had to be been demolished[13]. Türnich has survived because of its architectural merit, and it has the backing of the state government and the National  Foundation for Monument Protection[14]. The family are working on a rescue plan but it's hard to see how an easy solution will be found.

After the abolition of the electorate of Cologne, Augustusburg had a chequered history. Napoleon gave it to Marshal Davout, who never lived there. King Friedrich Wilhelm IV of Prussia renovated it before Queen Victoria's visit, but later Prussian kings and emperors took little interest and rarely visited. Falkenlust was bought by a rich family of brewers in 1830 and stayed in private ownership until it was bought back by the state in 1960. After the fall of the German monarchy in 1918 Augustusburg became a museum. Its fate was uncertain after World War II but changed dramatically for the better when nearby Bonn became the capital of the new Federal Republic of Germany (West Germany). Augustusburg was the venue for the inauguration of the first Federal President in 1949 and over the next nearly fifty years, until 1996, it was host to almost one hundred state visits and other official receptions. When Queen Elizabeth II made her first state visit in May 1965 she was given the same honour as her great-great-grandmother, Queen Victoria, of a *Great Tattoo* at Augustusburg[15]. When she came on her third state visit in October 1992, she gave the president a book of reproductions of the watercolours of the schloss that Friedrich Wilhelm IV had given to Victoria nearly one hundred and fifty years before[16].

Nordkirchen

Schloss Nordkirchen in Westphalia was built by Graf Ferdinand von Plettenberg, who was Clemens August's prime minister and played a key role in getting all those church appointments for him. Ferdinand had a very rapid rise in the world; followed by an even quicker fall. Nordkirchen was the outward manifestation of his success, but in the end he lost it.

Nordkirchen is often called the *Versailles of Westphalia* due to its large size and stately appearance, and also because it was inspired by French architecture. Built of red brick and white sandstone, the schloss is on a rectangular island surrounded by a wide moat, and outside of that a canal. Each corner of the island is accentuated by a small free-standing pavilion. One of these houses the information office, where we got a very warm welcome.

The schloss is owned by the state of North Rhine-Westphalia and is home to their Fachhochschule für Finanzen or training college for tax inspectors. We arrived at the beginning of the college day and there

6. Schloss Nordkirchen is known as the *Versailles of Westphalia*.

were students everywhere – finishing their breakfast in the refectory, parking their bicycles, and generally milling around before classes began. Nordkirchen has been in state ownership for more than fifty years and as a result is beautifully maintained. This is usually the upside of government ownership (access to funding); the downside is that interiors often need to be altered so that the schloss can be put to use. But there is still a suite of historic rooms at Nordkirchen, and these can be seen on certain days of the week. Unfortunately our visit did not coincide with a tour, so we spent a happy couple of hours looking around the outside and the gardens. There was information in English available at the tourist office, so we also found out about Ferdinand von Plettenberg's story.

In 1711, an ambitious young man inherited the Nordkirchen estate. Ferdinand von Plettenberg was twenty-two years old and at the start of his career. The estate had only come into his family a few years before when it was bought by Ferdinand's uncle, who began building a new schloss on the site. Ferdinand ordered the work to continue and the building of Schloss Nordkirchen is closely associated with his rise in the world[17].

7. The Vestibule in the suite of historic rooms at Nordkirchen.

Ferdinand's career began in the service of another uncle, who was the prince-bishop of nearby Münster. After this uncle died in 1719, it was Ferdinand who persuaded the cathedral authorities to appoint Clemens August in his place (see Augustusburg for the full story). Ferdinand's diplomatic skill also later secured further positions for his patron. In return Clemens August rewarded Ferdinand with advancement. He was made grand chamberlain in 1719 and in 1723, at the age of thirty-three, the prime minister of Clemens August's states. His power and political influence continued to increase; the following year, in 1724, he was made an imperial count (graf) and in 1732 the Holy Roman emperor gave him further lands and the highest decoration of the House of Hapsburg, the Order of the Golden Fleece[18].

As Ferdinand's career progressed, the building work at Nordkirchen continued. He remodelled the gardens, extended the buildings, lavishly decorated the interiors using designers from Augustusburg, and built up his art collection. The cost of it all was a quarter of a million thaler (an old currency unit). It is virtually impossible to put a present-day value on this sum but, on a very rough estimate, it could be around fifteen million euros[19]. A contemporary commented on

...the splendour of his Nordkirchen Palace, where everything is outstanding and reminiscent of a princely residence. Moreover, Count Plettenberg beautifies his estate constantly... [20]

But, as so often happens, Ferdinand von Plettenberg's spectacular rise was followed by a swift fall. It started with a disagreement about quite a trivial matter. In May 1733, after a hunt, there was a dinner in Jagdschloss Falkenlust at Brühl. During the meal a quarrel erupted over how the horses were stabled. Things got out of hand – insults were traded resulting in a duel, and Johann von Rolle, an adviser to Clemens August, was killed[21]. Clemens August was deeply upset over the death of his official. His killer was a relative of Ferdinand, and court rumour accused him of being behind the duel. He was dismissed from all his offices, banned from court, and forced to leave Nordkirchen in disgrace. His fortunes never recovered and he died in 1737.

After the fall of his prime minister, Clemens August was free to follow a different approach in his foreign policy. Ferdinand had been a loyal supporter of the emperor but from now on Clemens August would switch his allegiance back and forth between the main powers, so that the emperor gave him the nickname of a 'vraie girouette' (a true weather vane)[22]. It kept the peace in his territories however, and the large subsidies he extracted for changing his

8. The front of Nordkirchen seen through grand entrance gates.

support were useful for his many building projects[23]!

Nordkirchen has the most wonderful setting. I bought a poster showing an aerial view and have since looked at this many times with pleasure. Everything is rectangular and symmetrical, and surrounded by water. The entrance is across a wide moat and down a long drive, through three sets of grand gates, to the main building on the far side

of the schloss island. This is flanked by side wings, which mirror each other in an angular pattern down the sides of the island. The latest to be built were added just prior to World War I, to further grandify the schloss in preparation for a visit by Kaiser Wilhelm II. I particularly liked the two older clock-tower wings, on either side of a gaily-coloured circular bed of yellow and blue pansies.

Behind the schloss, connected to it by a bridge, is Venus Island where there is a garden created by a later owner of Nordkirchen. The duke of Arenberg, whose family were wealthy from mining rights, bought

9. Each corner of the schloss island at Nordkirchen is accentuated by a small corner pavilion.

Nordkirchen in the early twentieth century and spent large amounts on it in anticipation of the kaiser's visit[24]. Venus Island is a formal baroque garden with intricate patterns of box hedging, topiary, statues, and gravel paths. We enjoyed wandering around this in the spring sunshine.

Bensberg

In North Rhine-Westphalia we stayed in Schloss Bensberg, which is now an Althoff Grand Hotel. The schloss is in what was once the duchy of Berg, ruled by the branch of the Wittelsbach family who (in 1777) succeeded Clemens August's family as electors of Bavaria. But before that (in 1685) they became electors of the Palatine, and in 1705 Elector Johann Wilhelm II of the Palatine began to build Schloss Bensberg.

Johann Wilhelm wanted a really grand palace to impress his second wife, Maria-Luisa de Medici, grand duchess of Tuscany. He was also inspired by the memory of his visit as a teenager to the court of Louis XIV at Versailles. He engaged an Italian architect and thousands of workmen and craftsmen; but Johann Wilhelm died in 1716, before the schloss was fully finished. The workers were dismissed, and the widowed Maria-Luisa returned to her home town of Florence. So the decline of Bensberg began as soon as it was built and it was never used as a royal residence[25].

One of the historical themes that cropped up several times during our schloss tour was how many of Germany's royal family lines died out, causing all sorts of problems over inheritance. Johann Wilhelm came from the Neuburg branch of the Wittelsbach family, who were winners in this genealogical lottery. Johann Wilhelm himself had no descendants, but in 1777 his distant cousin acquired the electorship of Bavaria (to add to that of the Palatine), after the family of Clemens August died out (see Augustusburg). Johann Wilhelm's wife, Maria-Luisa de Medici, was the last of her line, and there were no more Medici after she died in 1743. In her will Maria-Luisa left the vast Medici wealth, palaces, and works of art to the next grand duke of Tuscany and his successors, on condition that it never leave Florence. Many of these treasures can still be seen in that city today[26].

Johann Wilhelm chose a hilltop site for Bensberg, next to the old hunting castle used by his father. To accommodate his plans, he enlarged the size of the site using landfill. His schloss towers above the town of Bergisch Gladbach and has the most marvellous views across the countryside to the city of Cologne, ten miles away. It was a clear day and the twin towers of Cologne cathedral were clearly visible. But I thought it a pity that the views are partially obscured by a depressingly ugly concrete town hall, built in the 1960s (in post-war *Modernist* style) as an extension to the old hunting castle. After World War II this style of architecture was a deliberate break with the past. Unfortunately the town hall at Bergisch Gladbach is in a very prominent position.

10. Schloss Bensberg was built by Elector Johann Wilhelm II of the Palatine for his second wife – Maria-Luisa de Medici.

Bensberg has a pleasing front elevation, painted white and grey, with five pretty and unusually shaped lantern towers; rather like pepper pots. It was a nice touch that our room key had a miniature version of these as a key tag. The courtyard in front of the schloss has lawns and a fountain and along each of the side wings there is an avenue of lime trees, planted close and clipped tight, with tables and chairs underneath. The leaves were beginning to unfurl in a light green tracery, creating a living sun-umbrella. The hotel staff had only limited information about the history of the schloss, but on a stroll outside we found two plaques, each commemorating a different episode in its story. The first of these told us that from 1840 until after World War I, Bensberg was used as a Royal Prussian Cadet School.

The Königliche Preussische Kadettenanstalt were boarding schools which took boys from the age of ten and trained them for the career of an officer in the Prussian army. The original cadet school was established in 1717 by Friedrich Wilhelm I, the so-called *Soldier King* of

Prussia. After the Napoleonic Wars entry was opened up to sons of the middle classes, as well as the aristocracy, and further schools were set up in the territories that had been incorporated into Prussia. Bensberg (in the Rhineland, which was awarded to Prussia at the Congress of Vienna in 1815) opened in 1840, and Oranienstein (in the duchy of Nassau which was annexed by Prussia in 1866) in 1867 – see chapter seven for Oranienstein. Much of what we know about life in the cadet schools comes from accounts written by ex-cadets, both personal reminiscences and novels and stories set in their environment. Most of the historical material was destroyed in World War II by a direct hit on the German Army archives in Potsdam during an air raid on 14 April 1945[27]. The accounts written by ex-cadets paint a consistent picture of a tough and sometimes brutal regime.

Education in the cadet schools focused more on physical training and military discipline than on academic achievement. The rationale was that boys needed to be inured to hardship and toughened up for their future life as serving army officers. So conditions were spartan, and the food barely adequate. In the winter boys shivered in their unheated dormitories where they were allowed just two blankets. Hunger was a constant and the stories are full of incidents such as boys cadging food from the kitchens or scrumping pears. In the twentieth century pupils at Bensberg would chant

Wir haben Hunger, Hunger, Hunger, haben Durst;
Wir wollen Käse, Käse, Käse, wollen Wurst.

We're hungry, hungry, hungry, and we thirst;
We want cheese, cheese, cheese, we want sausage (Wurst)[28].

The hierarchy of the school was on military lines and the older boys were given considerable authority over the younger, which led to a culture of constant, and sometimes savage, bullying. New boys were subjected to seriously unpleasant initiation rites and there were ingenious tortures with names such as *Bacon-swallowing*, *Spanish Rack*, *Stargazing*, and *Brandenburg Gate*[29]. The revolting practice of *Bacon-swallowing* involved forcing a cadet to swallow a piece of bacon attached to a string. The bacon was then pulled out of the boy's stomach by means of the string and given to the next cadet to swallow.

The bullying was tolerated, if not encouraged, by the school authorities on the grounds that what doesn't kill you can only make you stronger. Many boys accepted it too, as a way of demonstrating their courage and stoicism and showing they were made of the right stuff. There were cases of self-harm, with cadets sticking needles into or burning themselves for the same reasons.

11. Bensberg in 1907 when it was a Royal Prussian Cadet School.

The cadet schools always polarised opinion. They were anathema to German liberals and there were various unsuccessful attempts to close them down. Bensberg was stormed twice – first by the citizens of Bergisch Gladbach in the revolutionary year of 1848 and again by red revolutionaries in November 1918. But most ex-cadets were firm defenders and support for them went right to the top. At the start of World War I half of the military elite surrounding Kaiser Wilhelm II were graduates of the cadet schools, as were Chief of the General Staff Paul von Hindenburg and his deputy Erich

Ludendorff. The schools survived Germany's defeat and the fall of the monarchy, until abolished by the Treaty of Versailles in March 1920. Bensberg then became a state school but only a few years later it changed again and became another elite educational establishment run with much of the same ethos as the old cadet schools. After the Nazis came to power in 1933 the education minister gave a birthday present to the Führer – boarding schools to train the future leaders of the Third Reich[30]. In 1935 Bensberg became one of the National Political Institutes of Education – known as the *Napolas*.

The arbitrary decision by Kaiser Wilhelm II to send his nephews to a cadet school, against their parents' wishes, was one reason for the bitter feelings of Princess Luise Sophie of Prussia (the boys' mother) against him. Luise Sophie was the sister of the kaiser's wife and was married to the kaiser's cousin. In her memoirs, published in 1939, she lambasted the (by that time) ex-kaiser for his treatment of her husband, herself, and their children, and said she wanted to publish while he was still alive so as not to be accused of going behind his back. In the book she devoted a whole chapter (called 'Our fight with Emperor Wilhelm II for our children: 1903-1904'[31]) to the sending away of her two elder sons to the cadet school at Naumburg in Saxony-Anhalt, on orders of the kaiser. Naumburg was the last of the cadet schools to be set up, in 1900. But for royal pupils the conditions were considerably softened. Like their cousins the kaiser's sons (who attended the cadet school in Schloss Plön in Schleswig-Holstein), Luise Sophie's sons lived separately from the other boys, in their own house with tutors and servants.

After World War II Bensberg provided accommodation for the allied occupation force. We found a second plaque, on the wall outside the gates, put up to say thank you from the Belgian families to whom, for thirty years from 1965, the schloss was a school and social centre. Bensberg was in an extremely dilapidated condition when, in 1997, it was bought by an insurance company that invested seventy-five million euros to turn it into a luxury hotel. The Althoff Grand hotel opened in 2000 and is a very comfortable place to stay.

Burg Vischering

Münsterland is the name of a region in Westphalia, to the south-west of the city of Münster, which is famous for a high density of wasser-schlösser, or water castles. Nordkirchen is the largest of these. We also visited Burg Vischering in nearby Lüdinghausen, which is much older, in a very different architectural style, and has been in the ownership of the same family for over seven hundred years.

In the thirteenth century the prince-bishop of Münster built a fortified castle (burg) at Vischering, to help defend his territories against the covetous eyes of other local rulers. In 1271 the prince-bishop gave Burg Vischering to his steward or 'droste', and the Droste zu Vischering family still own it today. Large parts of the prince-bishop's medieval structure were destroyed in a fire of 1521; the zu Vischering rebuilt it over the following one hundred years in the renaissance style.

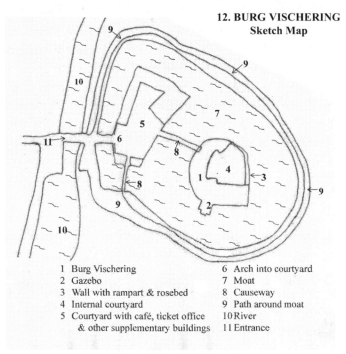

12. BURG VISCHERING
Sketch Map

1 Burg Vischering	6 Arch into courtyard
2 Gazebo	7 Moat
3 Wall with rampart & rosebed	8 Causeway
4 Internal courtyard	9 Path around moat
5 Courtyard with café, ticket office	10 River
& other supplementary buildings	11 Entrance

Burg Vischering is a fascinating example of a ringmantelburgen or fortified round castle[32]. To help me describe the layout I have included a sketch map as illustration number 12. The burg is in the middle of the moat and is almost circular in shape. Two-thirds of the circle is made up of the schloss itself (number 1 on the sketch map), and the remaining third by a curtain wall with a rampart walkway on top (number 3). We liked the sunny, cobbled courtyard this encloses (number 4), where there are several sets of external stairs leading to different parts of the building and a bed of roses along the curtain wall.

There are great views of Burg Vischering from the footpath (number 9) which goes all the way around the outside of the moat. The walls of the schloss rise directly out of the water and it looked like a little sailing boat. The builders of this water castle would have faced enormous structural challenges. The walls are built on foundations of oak piles, driven deep into the river bed. If the water level falls, these wooden piles dry out, and the structure becomes unstable. This happened at Vischering after two dry summers in 1911 and 1912. The problem was solved then by pouring concrete foundations, but medieval builders would have had to dismantle the walls, stone by stone and brick by brick, and rebuild them[33].

The entrance to Burg Vischering takes visitors across the moat and through the outer defensive castle (number 5 on the sketch map). This is a courtyard which now houses the ticket office and café, and other supplementary buildings. From here a narrow wooden causeway (number 8) leads to the schloss itself, where there is a museum about the history of the burg. Although everything was in German only, we still enjoyed this and some items needed no translation. We saw the stocks that once stood outside the burg, where miscreants were restrained by hands and legs, and a wicked-looking iron collar with spikes on the inside, dating from 1520, which was also used on prisoners.

The largest room in the burg is the sixteenth-century Rittersaal or Knights' Hall, which is used for concerts and lectures. This takes up the whole width of the building and is a light room from the windows

13. Vischering is a ringmantelburgen or fortified round castle.

on both sides. It houses portraits of the zu Vischering family from the eighteenth and nineteenth centuries. But most intriguing was the room with the oriel window in the Gazebo, that was built around 1620 and juts out into the moat. (The Gazebo is number 2 on the sketch map.) This room was intriguing because of a circular trapdoor in the floor set in a pattern of radiating floorboards, like the rays of the sun. Where did this lead we wondered? Was there a dungeon underneath? The museum curator didn't speak English and my husband has only limited German, but with goodwill on both sides we managed to understand the explanation. The fire of 1521 destroyed not only parts of the building, but also the castle archives and other valuables. So, when they rebuilt, the zu Vischering added a fireproof room for storage. This is accessed from the trapdoor which opens onto a spiral staircase.

The zu Vischering family moved to another of their castles in 1690 and for two hundred years, until 1893, the burg was empty[34]. During this long period it was looked after but never architecturally remodelled or altered, which is one reason why it is so interesting to visit today. Photographs in the museum show that, in the twentieth century, Burg Vischering was used as a home right up until the 1960s.

Burg Altena

The location of Burg Altena definitely has the wow factor! As we drove down the narrow valley of the River Lenne, along a road that hugs the riverbank, we could see the burg on the top of the steep valley side, high above the town of Altena. The only parking is at the bottom of the hill and it's a long steep climb up to the entrance. This schloss needs energy to tackle it, and is only for the hale and hearty!

Burg Altena was the ancestral seat of the counts of Mark, and the earliest records of it date back to the twelfth century. When the last count of Mark (who was also duke of Jülich, Berg, and Cleves, and count of Ravensberg too) died without a direct heir in 1609, there was a massive inheritance scramble among several claimants. In the end his properties were split between the descendants of his two sisters. Count Wolfgang Wilhelm of Neuburg (who was the son of the younger of the two sisters) got Jülich and Berg, and Elector Johann Sigismund of Brandenburg (the husband of the daughter of the elder sister) got Mark, Cleves, and Ravensberg. The sisters were eligible as claimants because of a family pact that allowed property and titles to pass down through the female line[35]. It goes to show why the royal marriage market was so tightly controlled and that the marriage of daughters, as well as sons, could establish inheritance rights.

So Altena became part of Brandenburg, later called Prussia (in 1701 the electorate of Brandenburg became the kingdom of Prussia). In its centuries under Prussian ownership, the schloss was used as an institution – first as a military garrison, and later as a prison, orphanage and workhouse, and as a hospital. Its future was secured early in the twentieth century when it was saved by the energy of two local men – Richard Schirrmann, who opened the world's first youth hostel in Burg Altena; and Fritz Thomée, who was the driving force behind the restoration of the schloss and the opening of the museum.

Richard Schirrmann was a schoolteacher who liked to take his pupils hiking out of school hours. One day they were caught in a severe storm and forced to take shelter overnight in a school. This gave Richard Schirrmann the idea of a network of hostels for young people that were a day's walking apart; that moment is regarded as the foundation of the youth hostel movement[36]. The first youth hostel (jugendherberge in German) opened in Altena in 1914, and the original rooms are still there and part of the museum tour. From the photo of the dormitory in the guidebook, it looks very similar to the youth hostels where I stayed in Switzerland as a teenager in the 1960s, except that we did not have straw mattresses!

14. Burg Altena is on the top of the steep valley side.

Fritz Thomée was the chairman of the county council who organised the restoration of Burg Altena between 1907 and 1915, and raised the money to finance it. Like many other old castles, Altena had been treated by the local people as a source of building materials for hundreds of years and was in a ruined state. The museum includes two models of the burg made in 1907 – one showing its condition at that time; the other illustrating the plans for reconstruction. There was a debate about these plans right from the start, with opponents arguing that Altena was not being rebuilt true to the original[37]. When a drawing dating from the 1690s later came to light in 1937, both sides of the argument claimed that it supported their position. But whether or not the rebuilding was historically accurate, Fritz Thomée rescued the schloss for future generations and it is a thriving place today, with the museum, youth hostel, and a restaurant.

After the reconstruction, the problem for Fritz Thomée was, as he said, 'having a castle that needed to be filled'[38]; so he set about collecting all sorts of things to go in it. As a legacy of this policy, the museum still has a wide-ranging collection and is organised into themed areas, numbered from one to thirty-one, covering subjects from the local rock formation, to how the aristocracy lived, to the history of metal wire making (a local industry). The museum visit is by self-guided tour following a 'rundgang' or suggested route through the rooms. This starts in the Commandant's Quarters (the building on the right at the far end of the narrow Lower Bailey or courtyard in illustration 15), which has themed areas one to four on the

15. The entrance to Burg Altena with a view of the Lower Bailey.

local geology. The tour then circles around the Upper Bailey (behind the Commandant's quarters) to finish in the Keep (the tall tower on the left), which was the final sanctuary in time of siege.

We began in the New Main Hall in the Upper Bailey, that is home to areas ten and eleven on the museum rundgang. These were the two rooms that interested me most as they cover the history of Burg Altena and the county of Mark. The first – a darkened antechamber – displays a fascinating genealogical table, dating from 1727.

The advance of Prussia

In 1417 the Hohenzollern family purchased a small and poor state in the north-east of the Holy Roman Empire called the Mark of Brandenburg. Over the next five hundred years they transformed it, through further territorial gains, into the mighty kingdom of Prussia. On the outbreak of World War I, Prussia stretched across the whole of northern Germany – from France and the Netherlands in the west, to Poland and Russia in the east.

The first gains came through the marriage of Johann Sigismund of Brandenburg to Anna, the daughter of the duke of Prussia (Prussia lay to the east of Brandenburg in what is now Poland). Through her mother, Anna also had a claim to her uncle's territories far to the west of Brandenburg, in the Rhineland and Westphalia. Both these claims fell in – after Anna's uncle, the last count of Mark, died in 1609, Brandenburg acquired Mark, Cleves and Ravensberg (see Altena); after Anna's father died in 1618, Prussia was added. Prussia was outside the Holy Roman Empire (and the jurisdiction of the emperor), and this enabled the Hohenzollerns to become kings. From 1701 the name of their state was the kingdom of Prussia.

The new possessions were detached from Brandenburg (Prussia to the east and the Rhine duchies to the west), and this drove the policy of future Hohenzollerns. They were unanimous in their determination to defend their existing territories and to add to them by joining up their scattered lands. This was achieved piece by piece by means of both war and diplomacy.

In 1740, soon after he came to the Prussian throne, Frederick the Great marched into Silesia (now part of Poland) and managed to hang onto this through three wars against Empress Maria Theresa of Austria. Further gains were made in the east through the carving up of the old kingdom of Poland at the end of the eighteenth century, between Russia, Prussia and Austria. Prussia was also a big winner when territorial boundaries were redrawn during the Congress of Vienna in 1815 at the end of the Napoleonic Wars, when most of the smaller German states were subsumed into the larger ones. Prussia acquired large provinces along the Rhine and in Westphalia, and a sizeable chunk of the kingdom of Saxony.

> *The last pieces were added in the 1860s as a result of Bismarck's wars. In 1863 Prussia and Austria defeated Denmark in the Second War of Schleswig-Holstein. Three years later Prussia turned on her previous ally and, in 1866, annexed the duchies of Schleswig and Holstein after defeating Austria in the Seven Weeks' War. The German states that had sided with the losing Austria, such as Hannover, Hesse-Kassel, and Nassau, also lost their sovereignty and became part of Prussia. Now at last, all parts of the kingdom of Prussia were joined together. Prussia was the dominant and by far the largest state in Germany, encompassing over sixty percent of both territory and population.*
>
> *After World War I, the kingdom of Prussia became the Free State of Prussia, which existed until taken over by the Nazis in 1933. After World War II the victorious Allies, being determined not to see any resurgence of Prussian militaristic values, dissolved the state and Prussia ceased to exist.*

The second room is the hall itself, lit by vibrant stained-glass windows installed when the schloss was renovated to commemorate three hundred years of Brandenburg/Prussian rule. The glowing red walls of the hall display a wonderful gallery of ancestral portraits, showing all the rulers of the county of Mark over a period of more than five hundred years. The first painting shows six early counts of Mark going back to 1398. The last in the series is Kaiser Wilhelm II, whose abdication in 1918 brought the German monarchy to an end.

From these two rooms we continued on the rundgang until we ran out of energy, and were defeated. It wasn't that the rest of the museum was not interesting – far from it. A lot of imagination has been shown in how things are displayed – area number fourteen, which explores the origins of old colloquial sayings and proverbs, is shown in a darkened blue space to represent the subconscious; and area nineteen, about tournaments, is in a tent with red and silver canvas walls using the colours of the counts of Mark. It's just that there was a lot to get through and the route was arduous – we went up and down narrow winding stairs and along walkways, and there was no way back or out!

Eventually we found a kind attendant who let us out through a fire exit, along with a group of school children and their teachers. The children were dressed-up, wearing medieval surcoats. Altena is a good place for children – there is a dressing-up area and they can take part in a special programme to find out how young squires learnt to become knights.

During our visits to Germany my husband and I see a number of schlösser in a relatively short space of time. To fix each one in my mind, I try to come up with a word or short phrase that encapsulates it and will trigger my memories of the visit. This is a technique that was explained to me by a friend who competed in the World Memory Championships. Using this system, Burg Altena will always be the *rundgang schloss*! Our final stop was the restaurant, which turned out to be one of the best on the trip. It has great ambience, with a medieval theme and suits of armour, friendly staff, and good coffee. Just the thing to top up our energy levels!

Detmold

Schloss Detmold was the residence of the princes of Lippe, who were rulers of a small state of the same name. The schloss was built by Bernhard VIII of Lippe in the middle of the sixteenth century, in renaissance style. The front view is dominated by a distinctive tower (see illustration 16), that I would describe as having the shape of a shell case or torpedo. The same tower is clearly visible in an old picture from 1633, that also shows the schloss surrounded by high ramparts and a moat. These were replaced by a park at the end of the eighteenth century, and the schloss now looks out on an open green space, where a fountain was playing. Everything was peaceful and serene, but Detmold was once the centre of a big legal battle over inheritance and the scene of a secret contract, concealed death, and surprise takeover.

I did not find out about the inheritance battle until after my visit. The guided tour was in German and although there was a handout in English, this said little about the history of the Lippe family. I do

16. The front view of Schloss Detmold is dominated
by a distinctive tower.

think that family portraits and historical stories are an important and integral part of any schloss visit; but so often curators concentrate only on the décor and furnishings. No photography was permitted inside the schloss, so I scribbled down names and dates from the portraits, and wondered who they all were. I had to wait until I got home, and could translate the material I brought back, to find out more about this interesting family. It was tantalising!

The big character in the family was Princess Pauline (1769-1820), who was married to Prince Leopold I. Her portrait was in the Elisabeth Hall; an elegant room dating from the beginning of the twentieth century and named after the wife of Leopold III. After her husband died in 1802, Pauline became regent for her small son and ruled the principality of Lippe for the next eighteen years. She doesn't seem to have been very keen to give it up, and her son (Leopold II) was well into his twenties before he took over.

The House of Lippe

The first documented member of the ancient house of Lippe was Bernhard I, who received a grant of land from the Holy Roman emperor in 1123. Bernhard had no descendants and it was his brother Hermann who was the ancestor of the house of Lippe, including its subsidiary branches.

The oldest of these subsidiary branches is the Schaumburg-Lippe branch, founded by Philipp, a younger brother of Simon VII of Lippe (1587-1627). Philipp's branch later became rulers of the separate state of Schaumburg-Lippe, not far from Detmold (see Schloss Bückeburg in my second book, Schloss II). In the next generation, a younger son of Simon VII, Jobst Hermann (1625-1678), also founded a separate branch of the family. This would itself later split into two – to create the different branches of Lippe-Biesterfeld and Lippe-Weissenfeld. Neither of these two branches had ruling rights.

The family were lords of Lippe until 1528, when Simon V took on the more important title of graf (or count). They achieved a further elevation in rank in 1789 when Leopold I was made a prince of the Holy Roman Empire and his county of Lippe became a principality. The family had apparently been after this move for several generations but could not previously afford the fees[39].

Lippe survived the process called mediatisation at the beginning of the nineteenth century, when many of the other small states in the Holy Roman Empire lost their sovereignty. It also avoided annexation by Prussia after the Seven Weeks' War of 1866, because Leopold III had chosen to join the Prussian side. Lippe remained independent and joined the German Empire on its formation in 1871.

In 1905, the main Lippe family line died out and, following a previous dispute, the inheritance went to the nearest related branch. This was the Lippe-Biesterfeld, who then changed their name to Lippe. The last ruling prince of Lippe was Leopold IV, who abdicated with all the other ruling princes in November 1918. The current head of house is Stephan, born in 1959.

Pauline was intelligent and also strong-minded; she recognised that for her small state to survive, she must reach an accommodation with Napoleon. So she travelled to Paris, paid court to the French emperor and made friends with his wife, Empress Josephine. There is a gorgeous tea-set on display in the Empire Rooms at the schloss which was a gift from Josephine to Pauline. As a result of Pauline's diplomacy, Lippe was able to join Napoleon's Confederation of the Rhine in 1807 and avoid the fate of many other small principalities that were abolished around this time. Pauline is also remembered for her social reforms to nursing and education; she opened the first kindergarten in Germany. She didn't have a very long retirement, dying just a few months after she gave up the regency.

Pauline's son, Leopold II, reigned until 1851 and was succeeded by two of his sons in turn – first Leopold III and then Woldemar. Their portraits, and those of their wives, are in the Hall of the Ancestors. This very large room (two hundred and fifty square yards) was decorated in the late nineteenth century in neo-renaissance style, and is meant to be impressive. Down each side wall is a row of carved wooden seats, rather like the choir stalls in a cathedral. Above them hang an uninterrupted line of portraits of the lords, counts and princes of Lippe, starting with Bernhard VI (died 1415), and ending with Woldemar (died 1895). It was Woldemar's death that unleashed the inheritance dispute. Neither he nor his older brother Leopold III had any offspring and the Lippe family had now run out of heirs. Well, not quite – Leopold II had a third son, called Alexander, but he was unmarried and mentally ill and had been declared unfit to rule. So the question was – who should have the regency for Alexander and succeed him when he died? This would be the subject of a bitter dispute. (Please see chart 2 for the disputed succession to the principality of Lippe)

The strongest claimant was Count Ernst of Lippe-Biesterfeld, from the most closely-related branch of the family. But what nobody knew was that, some years before he died, Woldemar had entered into a secret agreement with the more distant Schaumburg-Lippe branch, appointing Prince Adolf of Schaumburg-Lippe as the regent[40]. And Adolf had a very powerful sponsor indeed, because he was married to Princess Victoria of Prussia, the sister of Kaiser Wilhelm II. To take advantage of the element of surprise, Woldemar's death was initially kept secret. The gossip of the day said his body was kept in the ice-house until Adolf arrived in Detmold to take possession[41]. There is an old saying 'possession is nine-tenths of the law' and the idea was to present the Lippe-Biesterfeld family and the Lippe parliament with a fait accompli. The kaiser was accustomed to having his will obeyed and Adolf's mother-in-law (and Kaiser Wilhelm's mother) wrote in a letter 'William telegraphed to Adolf to go at once to Detmold, which he did.'[42]

But Count Ernst took his claim to law and the Lippe succession became the subject of a high-profile legal case. A special tribunal was appointed to arbitrate the claims, with King Albert of Saxony as president. Prince Adolf's side threw in every argument they could find; alleging that the marriages of both Count Ernst and his grand-father were morganatic and, as a result, the Lippe-Biesterfeld claim should fail. They did not succeed; in 1897 the tribunal ruled in favour of Count Ernst, and Prince Adolf and his wife Victoria had to leave Detmold. It was another sorry outcome in a line of disappointments for the kaiser's sister. First her brother had prevented her from marrying the man she loved (Victoria had taken Adolf as second best), then she failed to have children, and now she lost a useful role in life as the wife of a ruling prince. In the same letter her mother wrote

> It is a crushing blow for Vicky and Adolf. That charming home, lovely country and fine houses, position, occupation, future, all gone! Poor Vicky is most unhappy in life, if only she had children she would not mind so much[43].

So Count Ernst took over the regency and when Prince Alexander (the last of the old Lippe line) died in 1905, Ernst's son became Prince Leopold IV. There is a portrait of Leopold IV and each of his two wives

17. Statue of Count Ernst of Lippe-Biesterfeld outside the schloss;
Ernst was the successful claimant in the inheritance legal case
and the regent of Lippe from 1897-1904.

in the Red Hall, which is the first room on the guided tour and is named after the colour of the beautiful silk fabric on the walls. I was intrigued by his wives' portraits because of the big difference in their style of dress. His first wife, Bertha, died in 1919. In her portrait, painted in 1915, she is dressed in the corseted and tight style of an Edwardian lady, with accentuated bosom, narrow skirt, and the hint of a bustle around the hips. The portrait of his second wife, Anna, was painted in 1940. She has short hair and wears the loose and comfortable clothes of the 1930s, with a skirt cut on the bias to hang in graceful folds. Anna died in 1980 – more than sixty years after her predecessor!

Leopold IV was the last reigning prince of Lippe. When he died in 1949, he caused another family furore over inheritance when he overlooked the three sons by his first marriage and left everything to

Armin, his son by his second wife. It has been suggested that perhaps he did so because of timing. His older sons had been members of the Nazi Party and he feared that their property might be confiscated[44]. Armin lived at Detmold until his death in 2015, but his position as head of the House of Lippe was challenged by his older brothers.

The last portrait to mention was in the Hunting Room, where the walls are covered with antlers and other trophies of the hunt. This was of Prince Bernhard of Lippe-Biesterfeld (1911-2004), the husband of Queen Juliana of the Netherlands and grandfather of the present Dutch king, Willem-Alexander. Bernhard was a first cousin of Armin – his father was the younger brother of Leopold IV. Leopold and his children changed their name to Lippe, but his younger brother kept the Lippe-Biesterfeld name.

There is a very interesting history to discover at Detmold, even if this is difficult for an overseas visitor to access. I enjoyed my guided tour and walking through the fine rooms of the schloss. From the outside it looks deceptively small because what you don't see is that there are three more large wings behind the front, enclosing an internal courtyard. The tour goes round three wings; the fourth is still the family's residence. I clearly remember the moment, towards the end of the tour, when the guide threw open the windows of the Large Royal Hall to show us a view of the internal courtyard. This is absolutely stunning – how wonderful to look out on this from your windows every day!

Rank and titles

The size and importance of the German states in the Holy Roman Empire varied considerably and this was reflected in the rank and titles of their ruling princes. There were no kings in the empire and the highest rank (second to only that of the emperor himself) was that of an **elector**, who was the ruler of an **electorate**. So, as an example, Elector Wilhelm I was the ruler of the electorate of Hesse-Kassel (see Wilhelmshöhe in chapter six). There were only a small number of electorates and they were the largest and most important states in the empire.

Going down the hierarchy, a **duke** was the ruler of a **duchy** (for example, Duke Leopold I of Anhalt-Dessau – see Johannbau in chapter four); a **prince** of a **principality** (Prince Woldemar of Lippe); a **landgrave** of a **landgraviate** (the Ludovingian landgraves of Thuringia at the Wartburg in chapter five); and a **count** (graf) of a **county** (the builder of Schloss Pyrmont in chapter three was a count before his rank was increased to prince in 1712).

Many of these royal rulers craved an upgrade in their rank, and some were prepared to expend large sums to persuade the emperor to grant this. It is an irony that, after generations of lobbying, the Hesse-Kassel family only obtained the much-coveted elector's crown just as the Holy Roman Empire was about to break-up. The end of the Napoleonic Wars led to a general scramble for better titles. This is when some electorates became kingdoms (for example the kingdom of Hannover in 'Schloss'), duchies became grand duchies (the grand duchy of Oldenburg in 'Schloss II'), and principalities became duchies (the duchy of Brunswick, also in 'Schloss II').

After the fall of the monarchy in 1918, former nobility was no longer recognised under the Weimar Constitution. Since that time, royal titles have only been permitted as part of a surname – so, taking the house of Lippe as an example it is correct to say Stephan Prinz zur Lippe (Stephan Prince of Lippe) and not Prince Stephan of Lippe.

3

LOWER SAXONY
AND THE PRINCES OF
WALDECK-PYRMONT

Lower Saxony stretches from the North Sea coast and the border
with the Netherlands right into the centre of Germany. In the
days of the monarchy it was made up of several royal states, and there
are schlösser from all of them in my books, including the kingdom of
Hannover in *Schloss* and the grand duchy of Oldenburg in *Schloss II*
(see appendix B for the list of schlösser in this state). In this chapter
we visit a schloss from a small principality that held territory in the
south of Lower Saxony, and became famous for the marriages of its
princesses; and another that was given as a consolation prize to a bitter
younger son, and deliberately had no land attaching to it!

We stayed in the elegant spa town of Bad Pyrmont which has a
history as a royal health resort. The town is set in a bowl surrounded by
hills, and the roads into and out of it are narrow and winding. We drove
around lots of hairpin bends with 'hold-your-breath' moments. But the
views were just amazing – miles of green wooded hills stretching away
with little villages nestling between the trees.

Pyrmont

A long list of royal guests who stayed in Bad Pyrmont includes Tsar Peter the Great of Russia, Electress Sophia of Hannover and her son George I of Great Britain, and Frederick the Great of Prussia. When Queen Luise of Prussia, who suffered from heart and chest complaints, came during the brilliant season of 1797, there were nine kings and eighty other royals on the spa guest list. She stayed at the Fürstenhof (Prince's Court), a few yards from our hotel. Luise died in 1810 at Schloss Hohenzieritz in Mecklenburg, aged thirty-four (see *Schloss II*). There is a statue of her, carved from white Carrara marble, in the Strolling Hall at Bad Pyrmont, next to the mineral springs.

18. Schloss Pyrmont was the summer residence of the princes of Waldeck-Pyrmont.

Our hotel, called the Steigenberger Bad Pyrmont, was built in 1912 on the site of the old Kurhaus (principal spa building) which had burned down the year before. We had wonderful views from our window across the Kurpark (spa garden), which goes back to the seventeenth century and is still set out in baroque style, with avenues of hundreds of luxuriant palm trees in pots, and geometric beds of colourful flowers. There was a fete taking place in the Kurpark called the *Land-partie* during our stay and the Kurpark was a riot of little round tents with all sorts of goods for sale.

The principality of Waldeck-Pyrmont

The origins of the principality of Waldeck-Pyrmont start with the county of Waldeck and go back to at least the thirteenth century and the first-named count of Waldeck, Adolf I, who died in 1270. Pyrmont was added in 1625, through an inheritance, and the counts' domains then became the county of Waldeck-Pyrmont. In 1712 the count, who was then Friedrich Anton Ulrich, was elevated in rank to a prince, so that Waldeck-Pyrmont became a principality. Friedrich Anton Ulrich was the builder of the new schloss at Pyrmont.

Waldeck-Pyrmont was one of the smaller German principalities – in 1905 it had a population of 59,000[1]. But it survived up to the end of the monarchy in 1918, due to the far-sightedness of Georg II (1789-1845). He recognised that his small state was too weak to stand alone and hitched his wagon to Prussia, rather than looking south to Austria as his predecessors had done[2].

His son, Georg Viktor (1831-1893), continued his father's policies. By 1867, after the Seven Weeks' War, Prussian territorial gains meant that Waldeck-Pyrmont was entirely surrounded by this powerful neighbour. Georg Viktor suggested that Prussia annex his state, but Bismarck preferred to leave Waldeck-Pyrmont some independence as he could count on their vote in the parliament of the German Confederation. So Georg Viktor signed a contract giving over the administration of his principality to Prussia, in return for retaining some sovereign rights[3].

The last ruling prince of Waldeck-Pyrmont was Friedrich (1865-1946), who was the son of Georg Viktor. The head of the house today is Georg Viktor's great-grandson Wittekind, born in 1936.

Early on a sunny but cold spring morning we walked to the schloss, on the other side of the Kurpark from the hotel. There was no-one about – just a lady feeding the ducks on the moat – and the schloss had a rather dreamy air. Schloss Pyrmont is not large (more like a villa than a grand palace) and sits on a terrace on top of the high bank on the other side of the moat. It's painted icy pink and white, and it looked very charming.

The entrance is unusual in that, after it crosses the bridge over the moat, the drive goes into a tunnel through the bank and underneath the schloss to come out in a courtyard behind (called the South courtyard). I have included a sketch map as illustration 19 to show the layout. As a result of this construction the schloss has two more floor levels at the back than at the front. In the courtyard, the drive then bifurcates, with a sharp turn to each of right and left, up steep ramps and round to the main door on the terrace in front of the schloss. I should not have

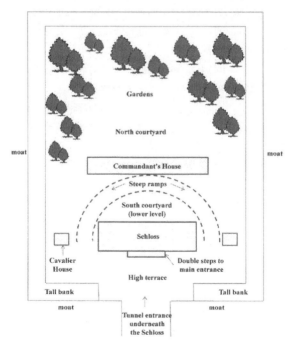

19. SKETCH MAP OF SCHLOSS PYRMONT

enjoyed going up or down those in a horse-drawn vehicle! Carriage accidents were as much a risk as car accidents today and the eldest son of King Louis Philippe of France died in a carriage accident in 1842.

Pyrmont was the summer residence of the princes of Waldeck-Pyrmont. Their main residence was Schloss Arolsen, some sixty miles away in what is now the federal state of Hesse, and the family still own and live in that today. The schloss at Pyrmont was built in baroque style between 1706 and 1726 to replace an earlier renaissance castle on the site, which had been badly damaged during the Thirty Years War (1618-1648). The new design fits well on a small site restricted by the moat. As well as the main schloss, there is another large building behind it, called the Commandant's House, with a further courtyard behind that (the North courtyard). And up at terrace level, on either side of the schloss, are the sweetest little cavalier houses I have seen. A cavalier house is a supplementary building which housed administrative offices and the royal household; they usually come in matching pairs.

Pyrmont is now a museum and has a permanent exhibition about the history of the spa. As this was closed for reorganisation we saw two temporary exhibitions instead – both very interesting but neither connected with royal history. Although we didn't find much about the history of the Waldeck-Pyrmont family at the schloss, we did have a most enjoyable visit largely due to a welcoming and helpful curator. I can't stress enough that this is the most important thing to get right from the visitor's perspective.

What I knew about the family before my visit was that it was famous for its daughters, and that one princess of Waldeck-Pyrmont became Helene, Duchess of Albany – Queen Victoria's daughter-in-law. I have always been puzzled by Helene's decision to marry Victoria's youngest son, Leopold, who suffered from haemophilia. He had previously been rejected as a suitor elsewhere because of his health problems. Helene would have been told of the likelihood that her husband would not survive long (he died two years later) and of the risk that the disease could be passed onto any children (their daughter was a carrier).[4] There was no mention of Helene at the schloss, but we found a portrait of her sister Emma, with a label which said that it was over six days at Bad Pyrmont in the summer of 1878 (28 July to 2 August) that nineteen-year-old Emma got to know her sixty-one-year-old future husband, King Willem III of the Netherlands.

20. Princess Helene of Waldeck-Pyrmont married Queen Victoria's youngest son, Leopold; this portrait is at the time of her engagement.

It is not clear whether the king came to Bad Pyrmont for his health or in search of a bride. But when he met the Waldeck-Pyrmont girls his mind turned to a second marriage. Apparently he was first interested in Princess Pauline (Emma's elder sister), but she was not keen on marrying an elderly widower and happily stood aside for Emma[5]. They became engaged on 29 September and were married at Schloss Arolsen the following January.

Pauline, Emma, and Helene were daughters of Prince Georg Viktor (who signed the administration of Waldeck-Pyrmont over to Prussia). There were six daughters in all – please see chart 3 in appendix D for their names and dates. The girls are never described as beauties. When Queen Victoria met the four eldest as children in 1860, she wrote (in a letter to her daughter) that their mother had 'such a plain, flat face' and it was 'a real misfortune' that the girls had 'literally no noses!'[6]. But they made very good marriages for princesses from such a small royal state. As well as Emma and Helene, another daughter (Marie) married the heir to the Württemberg throne.

At first sight, Emma's decision seems as puzzling as her sister's. Not just because of the age gap – Willem also had a reputation as an unpleasant man and a bad husband and father. His first marriage to Princess Sophie of Württemberg (who died in 1877), was a miserable disaster that poisoned the lives of their sons[7]. But Emma seems to have had a vocation and believed she could be of service as queen of the Netherlands[8]. She made a success of her marriage and everything I read said Willem 'adored her' and called her an angel. She became popular in her new country and her obituary claimed that 'Few dowager queens have been so much beloved as was Queen Emma'[9].

Emma's vocation was fulfilled when, on her husband's death, she was appointed regent of the Netherlands until their daughter, Wilhelmina, came of age. When King Willem III died in 1890 his only surviving child was his ten-year-old daughter with Emma, his three sons by his first marriage having all died before him (chart 4 shows the marriages and children of the king). Queen Wilhelmina was the first of three female Dutch monarchs in a row, spanning a period of over one hundred and twenty years. She was followed by her daughter, Queen Juliana (succeeded in 1948), and granddaughter, Queen Beatrix (1980). Beatrix abdicated in favour of her son Willem-Alexander (Emma's great-great-grandson) in 2013. But the next Dutch monarch will also be a queen – the eldest of Willem-Alexander's three daughters – Catharina-Amalia, princess of Orange, born in 2003.

The first of the two temporary exhibitions at Pyrmont was to celebrate ten years since the opening of the first children's hospice in Germany. A long and impressive list of celebrities had each contributed a signed sketch or painting, together with their photograph and a message. The name of the hospice (in English) is Lion Heart, and each picture was based on the design or shape of a heart. The drawing by rock musician Brian May, and his wife Anita Dobson, was of a large heart with the words 'Peace, Love, Joy, Freedom' inside. Donald Rumsfeld, ex-US Secretary of Defense, had contributed a colourful painting of a heart filled with the stars and stripes of the American flag. My personal favourite was the drawing by a famous British racing driver, Stirling Moss. This was a large number seven surrounded by seven little red hearts and a note to say that seven is his lucky number.

This exhibition was staged in the historic rooms of the schloss including the Tischbeinsaal (Tischbein room) or Golden Hall, which dates from the 1770s. This pretty room has windows on two sides and golden yellow walls, decorated with mirrors, colourful garlands of plasterwork flowers, and paintings by Johann Heinrich Tischbein the Elder (1722-1789). It is now available as a wedding venue – what a nice place to get married!

21. The Fürstenhof, where Queen Luise of Prussia stayed when she visited Bad Pyrmont.

The second exhibition was to commemorate the years after World War II when Käthe Kruse made toy dolls in Bad Pyrmont. Käthe is a famous name for doll collectors; she started by making dolls for children in her own family because she didn't think those on the market were realistic enough. After World War II, Käthe and her family fled from the Soviet zone and opened a workshop in Bad Pyrmont. The business was based here from 1945 to 1949. This small exhibition included display cases with Käthe Kruse dolls, and photos of her and her family.

Sieben Schlösser

Sieben Schlösser is the name of a group of seven (sieben) castles and palaces in the south of Lower Saxony (and in one case in neighbouring North Rhine-Westphalia) that are advertised together. This is a good idea because, although in different ownership, they are within easy travelling distance and it is possible to visit more than one in a day. The advertising brochure for the Sieben Schlösser includes a map and a table giving travelling distances.

Schloss Hämelschenburg was built around the turn of the seventeenth century and has been owned by the same family ever since.

Both the schlösser in this chapter (Pyrmont and Bevern) are part of the Sieben Schlösser grouping. It also includes Marienburg (built by King George V of Hannover) which is in my first book and Bückeburg (the ancestral schloss of the Schaumburg-Lippe family) from the second. The complete list is below, showing their location where this is different.

Bevern
Bückeburg
Corvey (Höxter in North Rhine-Westphalia)
Fürstenberg
Hämelschenburg (Emmerthal)
Marienburg (Pattensen)
Pyrmont

Bevern

The schloss at Bevern was built by Baron (freiherr) Statius von Münchhausen – nobleman, banker, and entrepreneur. In 1602 the widowed Statius married for a second time and decided to build a grand new schloss. He took a lease on Bevern, demolished the buildings, and the new schloss was built between 1603 and 1612. But soon after his financial empire crumbled, and in 1618 Statius was made bankrupt. He was fortunate to hang onto the schloss – only because his wife had residence rights. Statius died at Bevern in 1633. His widow (who was much younger) stayed on in difficult circumstances until forced to leave in 1652, when Bevern reverted to the dukes of Brunswick-Wolfenbüttel.

Today the schloss is owned by the local council and is used as a museum, café, and cultural centre. Once a week on summer evenings, after dark, they stage a *son et lumière* (sound and lightshow) in the courtyard, which tells the story of Schloss Bevern and of Statius von Münchhausen. We didn't see the show, as we weren't there at the right time. But luckily, a nice lady from the Friends Association, who was manning the museum ticket office, remembered that they have a summary of the script in English. It was a happy moment when she produced this, as there was no other information in English[10].

Statius was born in 1555 into an important and wealthy noble family. The only family member I had heard of before was the eighteenth-century Baron Hieronymus von Münchhausen (a descendant of Statius's brother) whose tall tales about his experiences were the basis of a famous book[11]. Statius was not content to live off the family wealth; he took his share of the inheritance when his father died and invested it shrewdly in business ventures. There is a large map in the museum showing his business interests – he was into agriculture, mining, and property development. As he got richer and richer and accumulated cash, he became a banker and loaned out money at interest, including very large amounts to the duke of Brunswick-Wolfenbüttel. Statius's problem was that he overreached himself at the wrong time.

Rapid inflation on the outbreak of the Thirty Years' War in 1618 meant that the duke's debts to him became almost worthless. Statius couldn't meet his own obligations and was bankrupted.

Bevern is a wonderful building. The schloss was purpose-built and everything is symmetrical – two main wings and two subsidiary wings enclose the courtyard, each with the same number and pattern of gables. This is a schloss that was built to plan, rather than being added to over the generations. The only elements that are not the same are the two staircase towers in opposite corners of the courtyard. The exterior of the schloss has not altered much from the original and is regarded as one of the best examples of the local style of renaissance architecture (called Weser Renaissance style). The local council is following a gradual programme of repairs and the front elevation has been restored and is painted back in its original colours of blue, grey and white. You can see a detail of the intricate carved stonework in illustration 23. The interior of the schloss however was lost long ago, after it was stripped out in the early nineteenth century to become a House of Correction. The nice lady from the Friends Association briefly closed up the ticket

22. Bevern is a fine example of the Weser Renaissance style of architecture.

office to give us a personal introduction to the museum and to explain the original layout, using a remarkable model dating from the late nineteenth century. This showed just how much of an innovator Baron Statius von Münchhausen was.

In its day, Bevern was a new development in schloss design. Statius intended to entertain on a big scale, but as well as grand reception

rooms he wanted comfortable guest suites. What was so innovative was that guests enjoyed privacy in their rooms, because the guest wing had a corridor. Statius's guests could climb the staircase tower and walk along the corridor to reach their rooms, without having to traipse through other guest bedrooms. Most schlösser were laid out *enfilade*, in a long line of connecting rooms, and this was the case in the family wing. But the guests had privacy, and even en suite toilets. The model showed a row of privies built all the way down the outside wall.

23. Detail of the intricate carved stonework on Schloss Bevern.

After the duke of Brunswick-Wolfenbüttel repossessed Bevern, he used it as a hunting lodge. In 1666 the duke, called August der Jüngere (the younger), died leaving behind three sons – two by his second wife and the youngest, Ferdinand Albrecht, by a third. At that time the usual practice among Germany's royal families was to split the family inheritance between sons. The practice of primogeniture, in which family property and titles are passed on to a single heir, usually the eldest son, did not become the general rule until the eighteenth century. So Ferdinand would have expected to inherit his own principality.

But his father's will disappeared and it seems that Ferdinand was stitched up by his two elder half-brothers. As his inheritance Ferdinand got only the schloss at Bevern and an annual pension. He didn't get any territory at all – his jurisdiction stopped at the gates of the schloss and even the village of Bevern, from which he derived his income, was under the authority of his brothers[12]. Ferdinand became a disappointed man, who felt he had been cheated and deceived. For the rest of his life he was in conflict with his brothers and when he came to write his memoirs, they were cram-full of recriminations and insults. Ferdinand set up a printing shop at Bevern, intending to publish, but this was shut down by his brothers who sent in soldiers to enforce their order[13].

But Ferdinand made the most of Bevern and during his ownership the schloss had its glory years. He transformed it into a princely residence, complete with theatre, library, art galleries, and pleasure gardens. Ferdinand travelled widely, bringing back paintings and art treasures to fill the galleries at Bevern. He enlarged and richly decorated the chapel, and eighteen princes and princesses were christened there over the next one hundred years. Ferdinand died at Bevern in 1687. He would probably have been delighted had he known that, nearly fifty years later (in 1735) his son, Ferdinand Albrecht II, would become duke of Brunswick-Wolfenbüttel, after the lines of Ferdinand's two elder brothers ran out of sons. (See chart 5 showing the succession to the duchy of Brunswick-Wolfenbüttel.)

After his death, Bevern stayed in Ferdinand's family, but never again achieved the same importance. By the early nineteenth century they could no longer keep it up, and Bevern was given back to the duchy of Brunswick-Wolfenbüttel. This is when the interiors were lost and it was stripped out for use as an institution.

In 1834 a House of Correction opened in the schloss, for men, women and children who had 'come to lead a life of immorality' and posed 'a threat to public order'[14]. This was effectively a prison and the regime was tough – inmates had to work for sixteen hours a day, and every aspect of their lives was closely regulated and supervised. It must have been a miserable place and the inmates tried to burn it down. Their mutiny was suppressed and the leaders sent into penal servitude.

In 1870 the House of Correction closed and was replaced by a Christian home for neglected boys and girls. The museum had a photograph of the children lined up in the courtyard on Sunday morning, the girls wearing white aprons to protect their dresses. I felt sorry for them and

wondered how much fun they had. In the Nazi years Bevern was a military barracks and after the war a refugee camp. When the last refugees left in 1949, it was in a desperate state of repair.

The village bought the schloss in 1957 and since then there has been a gradual process of bringing it back to life. There is still a great deal to do – we were allowed to take a quick look inside one wing which has not yet been touched at all. But today, Schloss Bevern seems a thriving place. Our visit was on May Day and there were plenty of people about. As we went into

24. The Maypole in the square outside Schloss Bevern.

the schloss, a tall wooden maypole was about to be hauled up in the square outside. When we came out, the festivities which accompany this were in full swing – with live music and lots of eating and drinking!

4

SAXONY-ANHALT AND THE ANHALT FAMILY

S axony-Anhalt is the first of two states in this book that were in East Germany (the German Democratic Republic) during the years when Germany was divided into two countries (the other is Thuringia in chapter five). In the time of the monarchy, before World War I, it largely comprised two different territories – the duchy of Anhalt, ruled by the dukes of Anhalt, and the province of Saxony, that was part of the kingdom of Prussia. (The province should not be confused with the kingdom of Saxony – see *Schloss*). At the end of the Napoleonic Wars the king of Saxony was forced to cede a large chunk of his kingdom to Prussia and this became the Prussian province of Saxony.)

After reunification in 1990, Saxony-Anhalt struggled in a market economy and unemployment was high. The population has been steadily shrinking. The state is off the tourist track for British visitors, and this was my first visit. Yet Saxony-Anhalt has a splendid cultural heritage and more UNESCO World Heritage sites than any other German state. We visit two – the *Dessau-Wörlitz Garden Kingdom*, a wonderland of royal parks and palaces; and *Quedlinburg Abbey Castle*, once a finishing school for the daughters of Germany's royal families.

Johannbau

The capital of Saxony-Anhalt is Magdeburg, but we stayed in Dessau which was the capital of the old duchy of Anhalt. The town is now Dessau-Rosslau, since it combined with nearby Rosslau in 2008. Our hotel, built after reunification, was modern and comfortable. We set off from there in search of Dessau schloss, the residence of the dukes of Anhalt and birthplace of the most famous prince of Anhalt. This was Leopold I, a great soldier known to history as *Der Alte* (the old) *Dessauer.*

It proved surprisingly difficult to locate. We found Schloss Platz (Palace Square), with a statue of Leopold I in the centre, but otherwise this was an insignificant square lined with ugly apartment blocks. Eventually we stumbled across what remains of the schloss tucked away behind the apartment blocks and hedged in by a major road.

The city of Dessau was almost completely destroyed by bombing in World War II. The imposing pre-war schloss (shown in the old picture in illustration 25) was badly damaged and after the war, with new infrastructure and housing desperately needed, there was no mood to restore it. 'Obstructive ruins have to get out of the way' read the headline of a local newspaper article in 1958.

25. Dessau schloss before it was badly damaged by bombing in World War II.

26. The surviving remnant of Dessau schloss, called the Johannbau,
is surrounded by post-war apartment blocks.

The purpose of historic preservation cannot be to preserve all
such ruins without regard for usability, or even to return them
to their former state. For instance, material and labour sufficient
for constructing 120 apartments would have to be sacrificed in
order to reconstruct the central section of the palace... The path
is free for the buildings of our socialist society[1].

The remains were blown up in 1960, leaving just a single medieval
wing, called the Johannbau. The schloss was once surrounded by its
gardens, but they went to make way for a new road and the surviving
remnant stands on a small piece of land. The Johannbau led a shadowy
existence in the GDR and had to wait until after reunification to be
restored. But it does look glorious now, although still cut off from the
town and cramped in by those post-war apartment blocks (described
in one book as 'unimaginative architectural pap made of standardised
slabs'[2].) But with the fall in population Dessau-Rosslau is a shrinking
city; the apartments are empty and gradually being demolished. In some
parts of the city the land is being returned to nature[3]. So perhaps there
will be another opportunity to think about the vicinity of the schloss.

The Anhalt family

The Anhalt dynasty goes back to the eleventh century and has the same distant forbearers as the House of Wettin, whose schlösser are included in all three of my books. The first family member to take the title of prince of Anhalt was Heinrich I, who died in 1245. Like the other ancient German noble families, before the practice of primogeniture was established, there were several divisions and reorganisations of the family lands between sons.

After the death of Prince Joachim Ernst in 1586 there was a major inheritance dispute between his sons and within a few years the family lands were split into five separate principalities – Anhalt-Bernburg, Anhalt-Dessau, Anhalt-Köthen, Anhalt-Plötzkau, and Anhalt-Zerbst (in alphabetical order). Anhalt-Dessau was the most important of these and went to the eldest son. In the dying days of the Holy Roman Empire, the German princes scrambled to upgrade their status and, in 1806 and 1807, the surviving Anhalt principalities were promoted to duchies.

The line of Anhalt-Köthen had died out quite quickly after it was created, in the second generation. Over the next two hundred and fifty years, three of the remaining four lines also died out, leaving Anhalt-Dessau as the survivor. Under a family agreement there was a type of tontine[4] so that each time a line was extinguished its lands went to the others. By the time the last prince of Anhalt-Bernburg died childless in 1863 everything had reverted to the duke of Anhalt-Dessau and his title became again duke of Anhalt. Chart 6 outlines the history of the Anhalt principalities, in simplified form.

Leopold I of Anhalt-Dessau was the son of Johann Georg II and was born in Dessau in 1676. His father had made a grand marriage to a wealthy Dutch princess, Henriette Catharina of Orange-Nassau, and she brought Dutch money, ideas, and expertise to his small principality. Leopold was a late baby and an only son – an older brother had died before he was born. His mother's elder sister, Luise Henriette, married the elector of neighbouring Brandenburg so Leopold was closely connected to the powerful Prussian court (Brandenburg became Prussia in 1701). He joined the Prussian army at seventeen, fought in many campaigns, and rose to be a field marshal. While on active service he formed a close friendship with his Prussian cousin, Luise Henriette's grandson. When his cousin became King Friedrich Wilhelm I in 1713, he put Leopold in charge of training the Prussian army.

Leopold transformed the Prussian infantry into a formidable fighting force. He was a strict disciplinarian who used brutal methods to instil obedience and discipline. But he was also an innovator who introduced *Marching in step*, a skill that had been lost since the Roman legions and which allowed columns of soldiers to manoeuvre more effectively[5]. Leopold was not just a drill-ground general; he has been described as 'a soldier of the blood-'n'-guts variety[6]'. He fought his last battle in 1745, aged sixty-nine, after Frederick the Great had called up *Der Alte Dessauer* in the First Silesian War. On the eve of the battle of Kesselsdorf, in which he won a resounding victory, Leopold is supposed to have prayed for success

27. Statue of Leopold I (*Der Alte Dessauer*) in the Schloss Platz in Dessau-Rosslau.

> Lord God, help me. Or, if you will not help me, then let us alone to manage it by ourselves and at least do not help those scoundrels the enemy![7]

Leopold's fame rests on his achievements as a soldier. But there are other interesting things about him. As a young man he fell in love with a commoner, a pharmacist's daughter called Anna Luise Föhse, and stuck out for marrying her against considerable opposition. They were married in 1698, when he was twenty-two years old. A few years later Anna was raised by the Holy Roman emperor to the rank of princess, which meant their marriage was recognised as equal and their children had dynastic rights. It was the dream of many a royal mistress or morganatic (non-dynastic) wife to become a princess (see the story of Anna's contemporary, Billa von Neitschutz under Rochlitz in *Schloss*), but Anna lived the dream. I asked how her husband managed it and was told he paid a large sum of money into the chancellery of the Holy Roman Empire[8]! The marriage seems to have been successful and they had ten children together. All the later princes of Anhalt-Dessau and dukes of Anhalt were descended from Anna Luise Föhse.

28. The Johannbau was restored after reunification and looks glorious now.

Leopold was a reformer in his home state. There he got rid of the local nobility by buying them out, and used Dutch techniques to drain the land and improve it for agriculture. The area along the Elbe and Mulde rivers, which ran through Anhalt-Dessau, is marshy. We came across an anecdote about him several times in Dessau. Leopold is riding through the town when he comes across a group of women selling pottery. After they complain to him that business is bad, he rides back and forth through their wares until every pot and plate are broken. The women are distraught, until he announces he will pay for everything and so they will have good business after all![9]

Der Alte Dessauer died in Dessau in 1747. We enjoyed our visit to the surviving wing of his schloss very much. The Johannbau is an attractive building in great condition, with interesting architectural features, and set off by elaborate filigree metal gates. It houses a café and the city museum but this was closed when we were there and we did not get to see inside.

Mosigkau

From the moment we arrived at Mosigkau, I knew I would like this schloss. I can't really explain why, but as we hurried through the grand gates and across the courtyard in front of the schloss, I had a good feeling. It was late afternoon, and when we arrived at the ticket office in the cavalier house this was shut, with a notice to say that the last guided tour had started five minutes before. Worse still, Mosigkau would now be closed until after we had left Saxony-Anhalt. Readers who have been to Germany may remember the bane of Mondays, when many museums are closed. In Saxony-Anhalt it is the bane of Tuesdays as well! But wait, perhaps all was not lost – we could see a small group of people standing at the bottom of the steps in front of the schloss, apparently listening to a guide. Margot (the guide) was initially taken aback when we approached her but kindly agreed we could join the tour. And so I got to see one of my favourite schlösser in this book.

29. Mosigkau was built by Princess Anna Wilhelmine of Anhalt-Dessau.

67

Mosigkau is a few miles south west of Dessau and is part of the *Dessau-Wörlitz Garden Kingdom*. It was built in the 1750s by Princess Anna Wilhelmine of Anhalt-Dessau (1715-1780) who was the daughter of Leopold I and Anna Luise Föhse (see Dessau Old Schloss). In the eighteenth century it was usual for princesses to be married very young, to a husband chosen by their parents for reasons of state – perhaps to cement a diplomatic alliance or establish inheritance rights. So I was intrigued to learn that Anna Wilhelmine did not marry, and no-one seems to know precisely why. It cannot have been that her mother's lowly birth disqualified Anna Wilhelmine in the royal marriage market (her mother was the daughter of a pharmacist), because her sisters did make dynastic marriages. Perhaps Anna Wilhelmine was looking for love like her father, or no suitable prince came into sight, or she just wanted to stay single. She is said to have been her father's favourite daughter, so perhaps he fell in with her wishes[10].

30. The oranges in the background of this portrait of Anna Wilhelmine are a reference to her descent from the Dutch princes of Orange.

31. The Garden Hall has paintings from the *Orange inheritance*.

Anna Wilhelmine was allowed her own income from state revenues by her father, and when she received a family inheritance in the 1740s she built Mosigkau as her summer residence. In the winter she lived in the Kleinen Palais (small palace) in Dessau. There are several portraits of her at Mosigkau, painted at different times of her life. In all of them, like the one shown in illustration 30, she looks directly out of the picture at the onlooker, with a self-contained and steady gaze. The oranges in the background of the portrait are a reference to her descent from the princes of Orange. Anna Wilhelmine's grandmother was the wealthy Dutch princess, Henriette Catharina of Orange-Nassau. (See chart 7 for a family tree of the princes of Anhalt-Dessau). When she came to Dessau as the bride of Johann Georg II in 1659, Henriette Catharina brought paintings, furniture and other treasures from Holland and these became known as the *Orange inheritance*. Part of it came to Anna Wilhelmine and is at Mosigkau.

The Gartensaal, or Garden Hall, is the largest and grandest room at Mosigkau, which takes up a large part of the ground floor and extends over one and a half stories in height. It was used to receive visitors and for entertaining. All the way down one side of this long, south-facing, room are floor to ceiling windows. The other walls are hung with Dutch masterpieces from the *Orange inheritance*, including Brueghel, Rubens, and Van Dyke. In the Gartensaal there is a portrait (on the left in illustration 31) of a young boy wearing a cap. This is Anna Wilhelmine's great-uncle Willem II of Orange (the brother of her Dutch grandmother, Henriette Catharina), painted by Anthony van Dyke in 1632. Willem married Mary Stuart, the daughter of Charles I. Their son, Willem III, married another Mary Stuart, (the daughter of James II) and they became joint monarchs of England (William and Mary) in 1688, when James II was overthrown.

There are other Stuart references at Mosigkau. The Brown Cabinet (Braunes Kabinett) was the private sanctuary of Anna Wilhelmine and connects her living rooms with the Garden Hall. This small but

gorgeous room is panelled with alder and pear wood and still has its original furnishings. The walls are hung with a so-called *Gallery of Beauties* – twelve portraits of ladies at the court of Charles I of England; copies of the Van Dyke originals by an assistant in his studio.

It seems strange to say this about a schloss, but Mosigkau is homely. The interior is richly decorated and steeped in history; but it is not intimidating. From the time we stepped through the front door I felt this was a house that could be lived in, and another visitor on our tour said this too. When she died in 1780, Anna Wilhelmine left Mosigkau to a charity to provide a home for

32. The Brown Cabinet has a *Gallery of Beauties* – portraits of ladies at the court of Charles I.

impoverished ladies from the Anhalt aristocracy (the *Hochadeligen Fräuleinstiftes zu Mosigkau*). She set everything up before she died and chose the first lady supervisor. Rooms were divided to provide living accommodation for the ladies, and some of these have been left as they were, and are included in the guided tour. The charity continued to exist and carried out her wishes until 1945, since when the schloss has been a museum. And the last of the impoverished ladies lived on in her rooms at Mosigkau until she died in 1968.

I liked everything about Mosigkau. It is not the most beautiful building in this book, nor the best maintained – the orange-coloured paint on the outside of the building was peeling and the gardens rather neglected. But Mosigkau was a special place; it had a purposeful and serene air – rather like Anna Wilhelmine in her portraits. The tour was in German but our guide was kind and found time to give us a few words in English in each room; other visitors also helped out with translation. Afterwards Margot sent me the unofficial English text of the tour, that helped me to write this piece[11]. I would like to go back to Mosigkau again and find out more about Anna Wilhelmine's story.

Wörlitz Country House

I was initially confused about the identity of Prince Franz of Anhalt-Dessau. There were references to him everywhere in Dessau – as the creator of the *Dessau-Wörlitz Garden Kingdom*, the builder of Wörlitz Country House, and as a great benefactor to his principality. But where was he on the Anhalt-Dessau family tree? I did eventually work it out – Prince Leopold III Friedrich Franz (1740-1817) was the grandson of the *Alte Dessauer* and the longest reigning prince of Anhalt-Dessau. He succeeded his father at eleven-years-old and died aged seventy-six. Leopold III is never referred to by his proper name, but always as just Prince Franz or, even more affectionately, as *Vater Franz* (Father Franz). Please see chart 7 in appendix D for a family tree for the princes of Anhalt-Dessau.

The Dessau-Wörlitz Garden Kingdom

The Dessau-Wörlitz Garden Kingdom is an ensemble of palaces and royal parks around Dessau-Rosslau and Wörlitz in Saxony-Anhalt, and is a World Heritage Site. It was created by Prince Franz of Anhalt-Dessau (1740-1817) with the idea of combining nature, architecture and people in a harmonious way. The prince was influenced by English ideas and laid out an English landscape park incorporating his family schlösser. When the great German writer Johann Wolfgang von Goethe (1747-1832) visited he said

Now it is supremely beautiful here; last night as we travelled through the lakes, canals and spinneys I was deeply moved to think how the gods have allowed the prince to create a dream around himself...it is like an unfolding fairy-tale...[12]

Wörlitz Country House (built by Prince Franz) and Mosigkau (built by his aunt) are part of the Garden Kingdom. We also visited the gardens at two of the other schlösser in the kingdom – Luisium and Oranienbaum.

In the 1770s, Prince Franz built a small schloss (schlösschen) near Dessau as a retreat for his wife, Princess Luise of Brandenburg-Schwedt. This is called Luisium after her and it's where Prince Franz died, following a fall from his horse. Everything was coming into leaf in the landscape park around Luisium, and it was the perfect place to wander on a spring afternoon. The schloss itself reminded me of an old-fashioned tea-caddy. It stands on a hillock above a narrow winding lake, and there were marvellous views of it from different places in the park.

Oranienbaum, south east of Dessau, is older, larger, and more formal. This schloss was built in the 1680s by Henriette Catherina, princess of Orange, the mother of the old Dessauer. Her father had four daughters who all married German princes and all built a schloss in Germany with 'orange' in its name. We will see another, called Oranienstein, in chapter seven. I liked the formality of the gardens, with canals, topiary, and expanse of lawn, and also the large orangeries on the south side of the park.

33. The Country House at Wörlitz was the first building in Germany
in the new classical style.

Prince Franz started his reign under the regency of his uncle, but as soon as he could he changed things in Anhalt-Dessau. He resigned from the Prussian army, ending a long tradition of military service to the Prussian throne that had started with his great-grandfather, and he took his country out of the Seven Years War (1756-1763). He wanted to follow a different course to Prussia in his principality. Anhalt-Dessau was a small state (in Prince Franz's time about seven hundred square kilometres and around thirty thousand inhabitants[13]), and breaking away from Prussia wasn't trouble-free. The king of Prussia was Frederick the Great and he was not best pleased. He extracted a heavy toll in return, in the form of grain, horses, recruits, and money, which almost brought little Anhalt-Dessau to its knees[14]. Frederick also arranged for Prince Franz to marry his niece, Princess Luise of Brandenburg-Schwedt. It did not turn out to be a happy marriage.

After the Seven Years War, Prince Franz went on a European trip, with his bosom friend, who was also his closest adviser and his architect, Friedrich-Wilhelm von Erdmannsdorff. They came back with heads full of the architecture of Ancient Greece and Rome, and of the new English style of landscape gardening. Prince Franz began to create one of the earliest and largest landscape parks in Germany at Wörlitz and, in 1769, he laid the foundation stone for a schloss called the Wörlitz Landhaus, or Wörlitz Country House.

34. Wörlitz from the air, showing the Country House and the lake behind.

Wörlitz Park extends over two hundred and seventy acres. It has a large lake (the Wörlitzer See) in the middle and is dotted with buildings, follies, and statues. Prince Franz was an enlightened ruler and the park was open to the public from the beginning. We were there at the weekend and it was heaving with local people out enjoying themselves in the spring sunshine – walking the paths, queuing up to be rowed in gondolas on the lake, and crowding into the café. But there were only four of us on the guided tour of the Country House and it was quiet inside. During our time in Dessau we did not come across another English visitor, and we were a bit of a novelty. The tour guide sent a message to her teenage daughter, who turned up with a friend half-way through the tour, to practice their English!

The Country House was the first building in Germany to be built in the new, uncluttered, classical style that takes its inspiration from the architecture of antiquity and the sixteenth-century Venetian architect, Andrea Palladio. The first room on the tour was the circular entrance hall, filled by a large statue in the centre. This is a copy of the *Apollo of the Belvedere*, a famous sculpture from Ancient Rome.

Prince Franz built the Country House as an expression of the new ideas he had absorbed on his travels abroad. He saw it as an educational tool to introduce his people to art, philosophy, and new thinking[15]. It was always more of a museum than a family home and I was not surprised that both he and his wife preferred to stay elsewhere. Princess Luise lived in the Princess's or Grey House, a pretty building behind the Country House and next to the church (she was devout). Prince Franz himself retreated to the Gothic House on the other side of the lake, where he lived with the gardener's daughter, Luise Schoch, the mother of three of his illegitimate children (three daughters)[16].

But there are more hints of the prince's personality at the Wörlitz Country House than of his wife's. The Princess's bedroom is an impressive but impersonal space; dominated by the state bed which is raised on a dais in an alcove at one side. On the bedhead is a black Wedgewood figure of a sleeping boy, which is a symbol for sleep. This is one of the largest pieces ever produced by the English Wedgewood factory. In contrast, the Prince's bedroom, a few rooms away, has favourite souvenirs from his trips abroad and a novelty bed which converts into a desk. Prince Franz designed this himself and was clearly an inventive man. In the Banqueting Hall there is another of his devices – a cunningly concealed pull down bed to accommodate guests that looks just like a door in the wall.

I love looking at family portraits because they illustrate the personal stories from history and also help me to fix family trees in my mind. So my favourite room in the Country House was the Dining Hall, which has a gallery of portraits of the Anhalt-Dessau family. Here were the four generations of princes, whose stories I so much enjoyed discovering through visiting their schlösser. They are shown on the family tree in chart 7. The first is Johann Georg II, who did a great thing for his little

35. The Dining Hall has portraits of the Anhalt-Dessau family.

state when he married a rich Dutch princess. In one of my old books I found a genealogical chart showing that fourteen of Europe's royal families are descended from Johann Georg and his wife [17].

Next comes the famous soldier Leopold I (*Der Alte Dessauer*), who must have shocked his mother (the grand Dutch princess) rigid when he insisted on marrying a commoner; and then his son, Leopold II, a shadowy figure who reigned for only a handful of years and had no influence on the history of his country[18]. The last of the four generations is Johann Georg's great-grandson Prince Franz, a benevolent and paternalistic ruler still remembered today in Dessau as *Vater Franz*. Prince Franz's only son died before him and he was succeeded by his grandson, Leopold IV.

This was my first visit to Saxony-Anhalt; with so many schlösser still to see around Dessau-Rosslau I know I will return there again. Because English speaking visitors are rare there was a dearth of books in English, but at Wörlitz I was fortunate to find one I will treasure. Called '*For the Friends of Nature and Art*', this is the companion book to a 1997 exhibition about Prince Franz's *Garden Kingdom*. I could hardly believe my luck when the curator suddenly remembered it and dived under the counter to get me a copy.

Quedlinburg Abbey Castle

But before we left Saxony-Anhalt, there was one schloss that I definitely wanted to see. So we drove sixty miles west from Dessau-Rosslau, towards the Harz Mountains and the town of Quedlinburg. The journey was quite an adventure because of the variable state of the roads. Our route switched from old road to new road, to road so new it was not in our Satnav or shown on the road map. We got lost; then tangled up in roadworks and a diversion; then lost again; until suddenly – we had arrived in the town and by a lucky chance at the schloss car park! And there, towering above us, was Quedlinburg castle hill.

The castle hill is a natural feature that has been enlarged by man; a plateau one hundred feet high and with an area of about twelve thousand square yards[19]. On the top of the hill, as shown in illustration 36, are the two towers of the romanesque church (consecrated in 1129) and in front of those, the sixteenth-century Abbey Castle with characteristic

36. Quedlinburg castle hill, showing the renaissance castle
and the towers of the romanesque church.

renaissance gables. At the foot of the hill is a delightful village of medieval half-timbered houses where we had coffee and cakes in a café before we climbed up to the castle. *Quedlinburg Castle and Church* is another of Saxony-Anhalt's World Heritage Sites. But the reason I particularly wanted to come here is that Quedlinburg Abbey Castle was once a religious foundation and finishing school for the daughters of Germany's royal families, and the centre of a sovereign state in the Holy Roman Empire that was ruled by women.

The history of the castle begins with Henry I (known as Henry the Fowler). According to legend, Henry was bird-catching on Castle Hill in 919, when the news arrived that he had been elected king[20]. Henry turned Quedlinburg into a royal residence, and when he died in 936 he was buried in a chapel on top of the hill, in accordance with his wishes. The present church is on the same site and Henry's tomb is in the crypt. Before he died Henry gave Quedlinburg to his wife, Mathilde, with permission to establish a religious order.

By the terms of the royal warrant of 936 setting up the abbey, Quedlinburg was to be headed by an abbess (rather than an abbot), and would not be subject to the authoriity of any bishop or local lord. It was an independent territory ruled by the abbess and subject only to the king or emperor. The widowed Mathilde supervised the abbey for its first thirty years and then, in 966, Henry's eleven-year-old granddaughter (also called Mathilde) was appointed as the first abbess. There would be another thirty-eight abbesses before the abbey was dissolved in 1803, and their names are a roll-call of royal princesses.

37. Medieval half-timbered houses at the foot of castle hill.

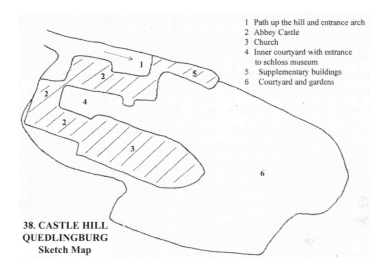

1 Path up the hill and entrance arch
2 Abbey Castle
3 Church
4 Inner courtyard with entrance
  to schloss museum
5 Supplementary buildings
6 Courtyard and gardens

**38. CASTLE HILL
QUEDLINGBURG**
Sketch Map

Illustration 38 is a sketch map of the top of castle hill, showing the location of the castle and the church. The castle (number 2 on the map) has three wings, one of which abuts the church (number 3). The wings enclose a cobbled courtyard (number 4) with a gallery running down one side, and this is where we found the entrance to the schloss museum. The first part of this is downstairs, in the older vaults of the building, and covers the foundation of the abbey and it earliest history. The second part is upstairs in the schloss itself, and this focuses on the abbey school and its abbesses in later centuries. The translation on the displays was patchy, so I was glad of the English guidebook and a short handout in English. But this is a wonderful museum.

The prestige of Quedlinburg Abbey was at its height in the first century after its foundation, when it was under the patronage of the four Holy Roman emperors who were direct descendants of Henry the Fowler. The schloss was a favoured royal residence, where the emperors made many visits, and the abbey was granted further lands and privileges. The position of abbess was also kept within the family. The young Mathilde (Henry's granddaughter) held the position for thirty-three years and was succeeded by Henry's great-granddaughter,

Adelheid, who held it for forty-five more. But Henry's line died out in 1024 and when the patronage of Quedlinburg passed to other families, the prestige of the abbey and the power of the abbesses dwindled. By the time the abbey was dissolved in 1803, its territory was little more than the castle hill and town of Quedlinburg.

In later centuries, Quedlinburg Abbey was both a religious order and a convent school which was so prestigious that the names

39. Before her marriage Princess Caroline of Brunswick was a canoness at Quedlinburg.

of daughters of Germany's royal families were entered almost from birth. A stint at Quedlinburg was a good thing to have on the CV (biography), and a guarantee of the impeccable breeding that was needed for a dynastic marriage[21]. Caroline of Brunswick, who would become notorious for her lifestyle as the estranged wife of the Prince Regent (later George IV of Great Britain), was a canoness at Quedlinburg in 1792, before her marriage[22]. (For Caroline's story see Braunschweig in *Schloss II*.) The pupils were called canonesses and could study at Quedlinburg until they married or, if they did not find a husband, remain as members of the order. The school curriculum seems to have been a mixture of academic subjects (such as Latin and mathematics), ladylike accomplishments (singing, calligraphy), and religious education. There were a number of salaried staff, including the abbess, her deputy (called the lady provost), the lady dean (responsible for discipline), and the lady scholastic (who was the headmistress of the school).

As befitting their rank, these ladies lived in style and we saw a suite of grand rooms on the first floor of the schloss. They include the Baroque or Blue Room, which was used as a sitting room by the canonesses and has portraits of several abbesses, including the thirty-eighth (and penultimate) who was Anna Amalia, the sister of Frederick the Great. Also the Throne Room or Audience Chamber, decorated in classical style with walls hung in vibrant red silk and beautiful white and gold plasterwork. This is next to the New Abbey with the abbess's private rooms; these were remodelled in fashionable Empire style in the 1790s.

There is little left of the original furnishings in these rooms as Napoleon's brother Jérôme auctioned everything off when Quedlinburg was part of his short-lived kingdom of Westphalia (see Wilhelmshöhe in chapter six). Instead, the curators have concentrated on the history of the abbey and the women who lived here – which to my mind was all to the good. An excellent exhibition called *Die Ideale Frau* (the ideal woman) told the stories of the last three women to hold the post of abbess before the abbey was disbanded. But it was the story of a fourth that really gripped me; of the woman who ruled the abbey from 1704-1718 but never became the abbess.

Aurora von Königsmarck was a Swedish countess, born in 1662. Her family were aristocratic, wealthy and well-connected; they owned property in Sweden and abroad and had links at the courts in Stockholm and Hannover in Germany. Aurora was beautiful, intelligent and well-educated. She spoke four languages fluently (Swedish, German, French and Italian), studied Latin, and was musical[23]. She had every advantage that high birth and wealth could bring, but by the 1690s things were going wrong for her. Her family had lost a lot of its wealth and property, and the elder of her two brothers died from disease on active service in the Hanoverian army. The head of the family was now her younger brother, Philipp Christof, and he was busy spending what money remained on gambling and extravagant living[24]. With her dowry gone, Aurora's marriage prospects were less glittering, and she began to lobby for a position at Quedlinburg to provide her with an income and security[25].

Where Till Eulenspiegel played a trick – Schloss Bernburg

The town of Bernburg is about half-way between Dessau-Rosslau and Quedlinburg, and we stopped there intending to visit the renaissance schloss. This was the main residence of the dukes of Anhalt-Bernburg (one of the branches of the House of Anhalt – see chart 6) until this line of the family died out in 1863. But the schloss museum was closed that day because of a medieval fair taking place in the courtyard. It was full of stalls selling craft items and medieval-themed food and drink, with the vendors in colourful costumes.

We were however able to climb the Eulenspiegelturm, the tall tower that dates back to around 1200 and is the oldest part of the schloss. This solid tower, forty-four metres high, is topped by a pointed roof with four gable windows that look rather like a hat. The tower is called after Till Eulenspiegel, a fictional character from German folk history.

Stories about the merry pranks of Till Eulenspiegel go back to medieval times and pop up all over Germany. In one story he is employed as a trumpeter at Bernburg when he plays a trick by sounding a false alarm on his trumpet. As the duke and his gentlemen rush off in response to the alarm, Till Eulenspiegel is able to gorge on their delicious dinner[26]. The town keep up the tradition of their connection and choose a child Eulenspiegel each year; rather as in the UK we would choose a carnival queen.

Since the schloss was closed we dropped into the tourist information office. They had nothing in English except, surprisingly, a short pamphlet about the last duchess of Anhalt-Bernburg. This was Friederike of Schleswig-Holstein-Glücksburg (1811-1902), who was the sister of Christian IX of Denmark (for the story of how he became king of Denmark, see Glücksburg in Schloss II). When she married the last duke, Alexander Karl (1805-1863), in 1834, Friederike apparently knew that he suffered from the mental illness schizophrenia, inherited from his mother[27].

His disease was progressive and from 1855 Duke Karl was confined under medical supervision and Friederike acted as regent. They had no children and when Karl died his duchy reverted to Anhalt-Dessau.

Then, in July 1694, disaster struck when Philipp Christof went missing overnight and was never heard of again. Philipp had been playing with fire by having an affair with the daughter-in-law of the elector of Hannover (see Celle Castle in *Schloss* for this story). He was last seen leaving his lodgings in Hannover for a secret assignation with her at the palace. It was never established for certain what happened to him that night, but the probability is that he was bumped-off on orders of the elector and his corpse disposed of in the river[28]. Aurora led the fruitless search to discover her brother's fate. His loss was a personal tragedy for her but also a financial catastrophe – Philipp was not officially dead so she could not claim an inheritance.

Aurora appealed for help to Elector Augustus of Saxony (Friedrich August, known as Augustus the Strong), the patron of Quedlinburg. He was an old gambling crony of Philipp who owed her brother money; so perhaps Aurora was hoping to collect these gambling debts. She became Augustus's chief mistress and they had a child together whom Augustus later acknowledged as his son. Maurice de Saxe became a renowned soldier and a maréchal of France. When the affair ended, Aurora retired from the scene gracefully and a grateful Augustus made a handsome severance payment (50,000 thaler[29]) and helped her to secure that much-longed-for position at Quedlinburg.

Aurora joined the staff in 1700 as the provost (deputy head) and the expected successor to Abbess Anna Dorothea of Saxe-Weimar, who was a family friend. Her appointment gave her an income for life and she was still free to travel as she was not required to live at the abbey full-time. Had she become abbess, this would have carried a higher salary and also the rank of princess. But when Abbess Anna died in 1704, Aurora found herself on the wrong side of internal politics and her appointment was blocked[30]. She continued as provost and, in the absence of an abbess, headed the staff for fourteen years. But eventually a new abbess, Maria Elisabeth of Holstein-Gottorf, took up the role in 1718. Aurora stayed on at Quedlinburg as provost until she died in 1728, worrying about money to the end.

Voltaire, the famous French writer and philosopher, called Aurora 'the most famous woman of two centuries'. There are portraits of her at Quedlinburg and a still-life painting that is supposed to be her work. Aurora also features on a genealogical chart that was the focal point of *Die Ideale Frau* exhibition. This was a family tree with a difference because, instead of tracing descent through the male line, it focused on the women whose stories were told in the exhibition, and traced the relationships between them. The chart showed love affairs as well as marriages, with the symbol of interlocked rings for wedlock and two hearts for a love affair. I was very pleased to find a smaller version of the chart on sale in the museum shop.

5

THURINGIA AND THE
DUKES OF SAXE-MEININGEN

If I had to pick my favourite part of Germany, it must be here in
Thuringia, which Germans call *The Green Heart of Germany*. With
its picturesque landscape of pine-covered hills and picture-postcard
villages, the Thüringer Wald (Thuringian forest) is the setting of
fairy tales. Before World War I there were seven small royal duchies
and principalities in this state, so that Thuringia is a treasure-trove
of fascinating schlösser. Nowhere else in Germany were the capital
cities of the dukes and princes so close together, or did they compete
so fiercely to display their grandeur and power through building their
beautiful schlösser.

This was my second visit to Thuringia and there are schlösser from
three of its seven royal families in *Schloss II* (see appendix B for the
list). This chapter includes schlösser from a fourth – the ducal house of
Saxe-Meiningen. We find out about the sad gynaecological history of a
queen consort of Great Britain, and a duke's love affair with an actress
in his theatre. But first we are off to one of the most famous German
castles of them all.

The Wartburg

One reason why schlösser are so fascinating is that they are places where history happened. Our schloss tours have given me an extra dimension of history to think about – not only who, what and why, but also where? A visit to the Wartburg is like walking through the pages of a history book; this is one of the oldest and most famous German castles, and connected with many important events in German history.

The Wartburg was founded around 1073 by Ludwig der Springer (the Jumper), ancestor of the Ludovingian dynasty. The schloss is perched on a steep spur of rock, two hundred metres above the countryside, and probably gets its name from an even earlier watch tower (Warte) here[1]. The site is narrow and the buildings are strung out in a long line – from the entrance gate on the north side (where the road winds up from the town of Eisenach), to the twelfth-century main building (the Palas) on the south side. The Palas is a remarkable feat of engineering. It extends three metres beyond the rock and is supported by a massive substructure, so that the building and foundations rise to an impressive height of nearly forty metres.

40. View of the Wartburg from a distance, showing the twelfth century Palas.

World Heritage Sites

A World Heritage Site is defined as a natural site or man-made structure which is recognised as being of outstanding international importance and therefore deserving of special protection². Sites are nominated to and designated by the UNESCO World Heritage Centre. UNESCO is part of the United Nations and the initials stand for United Nations Educational, Scientific, and Cultural Organisation.

The UNESCO World Heritage Centre lists forty World Heritage Sites in Germany, of which six are visited in this book. These six sites (in order of the book) are shown below. By no means all the sites in Germany are schlösser. The list also includes, for example, Modernism Housing Estates in Berlin, the Messel Pit Fossil Site, and Völklingen Ironworks.

Schloss Augustusburg and Falkenlust at Brühl (chapter two)
The Dessau-Wörlitz Garden Kingdom (chapter four)
Quedlinburg Abbey Castle and Church (chapter four)
The Wartburg (chapter five)
Wilhelmshöhe Park (chapter six)
The Rhine Gorge in Rhineland-Palatinate (chapter seven)

The fame of the Wartburg means it is very popular with visitors. The schloss was located close to the border between East and West Germany (just on the eastern side) and became a symbol of a divided country. In 1990, the first year after the Berlin Wall fell, 760,000 visitors took guided tours here and a million more came to walk around the grounds. There were plenty of visitors when we were there, of all different nationalities, and the Wartburg is an easy place to visit even if you don't speak German. They offer one guided tour every day in English but, as our timing did not coincide with this, we took the German tour with a handout in English. The handout was excellent and I really appreciated that, although comprehensive and helpful, it was small in size and easy to handle. At other schlösser I have been presented with large (A4 size) and heavy (laminated pages) documents, that can cause problems when I am trying to turn over the pages, take notes, look at everything, and so on. There is also a good English guidebook at the Wartburg and plenty of material in English in the shop.

The guided tour takes visitors through the Palas building which was built in the middle of the twelfth century (between 1155 and around 1172), in romanesque style. The Palas was the residence of the Ludovingian landgraves of Thuringia and some of the early chapters in the history of the Wartburg are connected with this dynasty. The Ludovingians were a powerful and well-connected family whose lands extended into both Thuringia and Hesse. (See chart 8 in appendix D for the family tree of the Ludovingian landgraves of Thuringia). In 1130, Ludwig I (the son of Ludwig the Jumper) was created the first landgrave of Thuringia by the Holy Roman Emperor Lothar III, in return for supporting his election as emperor[3]. His son, Ludwig II (the Iron), married the sister of the Emperor Friedrich I (Barbarossa), and in 1246 the last male dynast in the family, Landgrave Heinrich Raspe IV, was elected Holy Roman emperor after the pope excommunicated

41. An old picture of the courtyard with the Palas on the left (the exterior staircase no longer exists).

Friedrich II. Heinrich Raspe didn't enjoy his new position for very long and died the following year from an arrow wound suffered while he was besieging the city of Ulm[4].

By the end of the eighteenth century the Wartburg had fallen into a dilapidated state and the Palas was in danger of collapse. It was saved when Grand Duke Karl Alexander of Saxe-Weimar-Eisenach (the owner) decided to turn it into a national monument to German history, and restoration work began after 1838. The renovated rooms have romantic sounding names (the Knights' Hall, Elisabeth's Bower, the Hall of Minstrels), and are decorated with a nineteenth-century romantic perspective of the middle-ages. In the Elisabeth Gallery six frescos, painted in 1854 and 1855 by Moritz von Schwind, tell the life story of the most remarkable woman in the history of the Wartburg. This was Elisabeth, a royal princess and wife of Landgrave Ludwig IV, who was canonised in 1235 as St Elisabeth.

Princess Elisabeth was the daughter of King András II and Queen Gertrude of Hungary. As a four-year-old she was sent to Thuringia in 1211 as the prospective bride of the landgrave's son. The first fresco of the series in the Elisabeth Gallery shows her being lifted down from her horse as she arrives at the Wartburg. It is a charming picture and the little girl looks very cute – her face is framed by a bonnet and she wears a tight-fitting blue coat trimmed with fur. Queen Gertrude made sure that her daughter came to Thuringia with a dowry that would dazzle. A chronicler wrote that

...she laid her daughter ...in a silver cradle lined with exquisite silk cloth. With the child, she sent countless gold and silver drinking vessels, splendid fastenings, wreaths and circlets, much-decorated rings and bracelets, beautifully worked and with precious stones, many colourful ribbons and rich clothing of fur, cloths inter-woven with gold and baldachins... also one thousand marks in fine silver, ...and a silver tub in which the child was to be bathed. Such a rich treasure was never seen again in the land of Thuringia[5].

When she was thirteen Elisabeth became the wife of Landgrave Ludwig IV. But she never fitted the mould of a high-born medieval

lady and attracted criticism for her ascetic way of life and personal care of the poor and sick. The second picture tells the story of the *Miracle of the Roses*. Elisabeth is caught by her husband as she is leaving the Wartburg carrying bread for the poor. When he asks her what she is carrying hidden in her skirts, she tells him it is roses. The painting depicts the moment when she opens her skirt to show him, and lo and behold the bread has turned into – roses!

In the third fresco Elisabeth is saying farewell to her husband as he leaves for the crusades in 1227. He didn't reach the Holy Land but died from disease in Italy on his way. What

42. St Elisabeth and the *Miracle of the Roses*.

happened next is rather confused but Elisabeth's only son, Hermann II, was still a child and his uncle (her husband's brother, Heinrich Raspe IV) took over and forced her out. The fourth picture shows Elisabeth leaving the Wartburg with her children in 1228. Hermann II died young and all of his uncle's three marriages were childless so that Heinrich Raspe IV was the last male in the family. After his death in 1247 there was a long war over the succession and ultimately the family lands were split. Thuringia passed to the Wettin dynasty through Heinrich the Illustrious, who was the son of Heinrich Raspe's sister Jutta (Judith). The lands in Hesse went to Elisabeth's daughter Sophie who married the duke of Brabant and is the ancestress of the House of Hesse.

Elisabeth's charitable work was way ahead of her time. After her expulsion from the Wartburg she moved to Marburg (part of the family's landholdings in Hesse), where she opened a hospital and personally nursed the sick. This type of work was unheard of for a lady for hundreds of years to come. But Elisabeth's life was short and the fifth fresco in the Elisabeth Gallery depicts her death in 1231 at the age of only twenty-four. She was canonised just four years later in 1235, and the last of the six pictures shows the excavation of her remains after she became a saint. This was a great occasion in the presence of bishops and princes and the Holy Roman emperor himself. The appeal of St Elisabeth has endured over the centuries; many churches have been dedicated to her, hospitals and homes for the elderly called after her, and nursing orders established to carry on her work.

Another event in the very colourful history of the Wartburg is commemorated in the Festsaal (or Grand Hall), which was the last stop on our guided tour of the Palas. This is a huge room, which takes up the whole of the second floor. It dates from the nineteenth-century restoration by the grand duke of Saxe-Weimar-Eisenach and is lavishly decorated with paintings of famous members of the Ludovingian family. It was so admired by the Bavarian king, Ludwig II, when he visited in 1867, that he had a copy made in his fairy-tale castle of Neuschwanstein[6]. The Festsaal has great acoustics and nowadays is used for concerts and music broadcasts. Our guide played a snatch of music from the opera Tannhäuser by Richard Wagner, which is about the legend of a knights' singing contest at the Wartburg in 1206. It certainly gave the room great atmosphere!

The event commemorated in the Festsaal is the student demonstration and rally that took place at the Wartburg on 18 October 1817. After the Napoleonic Wars, many Germans were deeply disappointed that the old order, with its patchwork of royal states, was restored at the Congress of Vienna. One legacy of the wars of liberation against Napoleon was a liberal movement in Germany, calling for unification of the country and democratic freedoms. Five hundred students from various universities met in the town of Eisenach and marched up the hill to the Wartburg in the first democratic protest in Germany. In the

Festsaal the black, red, and gold flag of the student fraternity hangs over the chimney piece. These colours later became the colours of the German national flag.

Hotel Auf Der Wartburg

The hotel at the Wartburg is the work of Bodo Ebhardt, architect to Kaiser Wilhelm II and castle enthusiast. Bodo was the founder of the German Castles Association and the owner of Schloss Marksburg on the Rhine, that he bought with the help of the kaiser and where he lived until he died (see 'Schloss'). In 1891 he had spent his honeymoon at the old Wartburg hotel.

Bodo's new hotel has a staggering location, right next to the entrance to The Wartburg itself. In 1912 the rock was blasted away to create a small plateau eight metres lower than the schloss. The new hotel, in half-timbered neo-gothic style, was built in a year and opened in March 1914. I can best describe it by saying it looks like a real version of a Walt Disney village.

Guests arrive at the Wartburg Hotel on foot. We left the car lower down the hill and our luggage was ferried up by the hotel porter. This was the most expensive hotel we stayed in and, in my opinion, did not live up to its price. But the location is amazing and the views magnificent. From our window seat in the dining room for breakfast, high above the landscape, I could see out over miles of trees. There wasn't a house in sight – just dark green firs alternating with the lighter green of deciduous trees and an occasional grass clearing. As we ate, the sun came around and lit up the tree-tops. And the view was framed by a fringe of mauve blossom on the lilac growing next to the hotel. Magic!

By the end of our visit to the Wartburg my head was full of images and stories from the wonderful history of this schloss. It was a welcome interlude before we left, and a moment of peace, to walk along a narrow, covered wooden sentry walk called the Margarethengang (similar to the Elisabethengang in illustration 43, but shorter) to see a bare and simply furnished room in the Vogtei (Bailiff's Lodge). This is where the religious reformer Martin Luther took refuge, under the name of *Junker Jörg* (Squire George), after he was excommunicated by the pope and outlawed by the Holy Roman emperor.

The publication in 1517 of Luther's ninety-five theses against the use of indulgences by the Catholic Church was the starting point of the Reformation and the beginning of the Protestant faith. After his excommunication, the young monk was ordered by Emperor Karl V to appear in person at the imperial diet (parliament) in Worms in April 1521, to defend himself. When Luther refused to recant at the diet, the emperor placed him under the *Imperial Ban*, which meant he became an outlaw and his personal safety was at risk. He was given safe passage from the diet and on his way home a friendly patron (Elector Friedrich the Wise of Saxony) staged a sham attack and arranged for him to disappear. While his enemies thought him dead, Luther enjoyed a productive and creative writing phase under his pseudonym at the Wartburg. 'I write without pause' he said in a letter to the elector's secretary[7]. During his ten months in the Wartburg, Luther wrote the collection of sermons that he considered his best work[8] and worked on his translation of the New Testament from Greek into German.

43. The Wartburg from near the hotel with the Elisabethengang.

Elisabethenburg

What I remember so clearly about Schloss Elisabethenburg in Meiningen is the story of its music. The schloss was built between 1682 and 1692 as the residence of the new dukes of Saxe-Meiningen and music was always important here. Bernhard I (1649-1706), who became the first duke in 1680, enjoyed singing and music and was the founder of the court orchestra; a hundred years later Georg I (1761-1803), who played the flute and violin, opened this up to public concerts from 1781; and a hundred years later again, the most famous duke, Georg II (1826-1914), transformed the orchestra into one of the best in Germany that toured Europe from 1880 until World War I.

Elisabethenburg was hard to find. It was only after we asked directions that we found we had, without knowing, parked the car almost directly outside. The schloss is hidden from view by a long semi-circular gate-house building that connects the two side wings. Inside this enclosed space the schloss has a utilitarian look, with the façade painted white and the quoins and other stonework in contrasting

44. What I remember about Schloss Elisabethenburg is the story of its music.

reddish brown. The feeling of a cloistered world is reinforced by the views from the windows of the schloss, that look out onto its own courtyard and gardens with no glimpse of the wider world beyond.

The schloss museum occupies some fifty rooms over two floors, and the museum tour is self-guided using a hand-out of the floor plan and an English audio-tape (deposit of twenty euros required). Whereas the Wartburg was thronged with visitors, we hardly saw anyone else at Elisabethenburg – just the same couple once or twice in the distance. The museum is large and the sense of emptiness was exaggerated by the lighting system. To save energy, the lights were triggered on by movement as we entered a room, and off again after we left it. Looking to right and left down the enfilade of darkened rooms was eerie! The museum attendants were very helpful when approached, but largely distant and ghostly. For me the museum most came to life in the last few rooms with an exhibition called *Meiningen – Muse's Court between Weimar and Bayreuth*, which told the story of the court orchestra and the celebrated musicians who worked with it.

From the beginning, a series of accomplished musicians held the post of court music director at Elisabethenburg. They include the first director (1702-1707), Georg Caspar Schürmann, a gifted composer and singer; Johann Ludwig Bach (1711-1731), of the famous family of musicians and painters; and Jean Joseph Bott (1857-1865), who staged the first music festival and brought Franz Liszt to Meiningen as guest conductor. But the greatest years were from 1880, when the orchestra was under the leadership of Duke Georg II. During this period the music directors included piano virtuoso and star conductor Hans von Bülow (1880-1885); his protégé, composer Richard Strauss (1885-1886); and Fritz Steinbach (1886-1903), who was a leading interpreter of Brahms and made Meiningen into a Brahms centre. The composer conducted the premier of both his Third and Fourth Symphonies in Meiningen (1884 and 1885) and later (from 1891) composed four works for the Meiningen clarinettist Richard Mühlfeld, whom he called the *Nightingale of the Orchestra*[9].

The duchy of Saxe-Meiningen

When Duke Ernst I of Saxe-Gotha-Altenburg died in 1675, he left seven surviving sons. He wanted them to rule his duchy jointly, in a committee arrangement with the eldest as chairman. Of course this didn't work out, and the brothers embarked on a dispute that lasted for several years. When it was eventually settled, on arbitration by the Holy Roman emperor, the father's lands were split to provide a smaller duchy for each son. The third brother became Duke Bernhard I of the new duchy of Saxe-Meiningen. There were eleven dukes of Saxe-Meiningen before the monarchy ended.

The inheritance squabbles between brothers continued with Bernhard I's sons, and this is why the succession to Saxe-Meiningen looks complicated for the forty years after his death. I have tried to unravel and simplify it in chart 9. His eldest son, Duke Ernst Ludwig I, wanted to establish primo-geniture but was challenged by his brothers. The next two dukes (Ernst Ludwig II and then Karl Friedrich) were Ernst Ludwig's sons. Each succeeded as a minor and was under the joint regency of their two uncles – Bernhard I's younger sons Friedrich Wilhelm and Anton Ulrich. These two were on very bad terms and their rule caused chaos and endless difficulty. When Karl Friedrich died unmarried, the succession went back a generation. His two uncles ruled together until Friedrich Wilhelm died when, by virtue of living the longest, Anton Ulrich became the undisputed duke in 1746.

Anton Ulrich's problem now was that he was fifty-eight years old and did not have an heir. As a young man he had made a secret marriage that, when later revealed, was declared to be morganatic. This meant that his children were not eligible for the succession. After years of fighting, Anton Ulrich managed to have this decision overturned by the Holy Roman emperor. For a few years his marriage was equal and his children were princes and princesses, but the next emperor overturned the decision and Anton Ulrich was back to square one. His first wife had died and in 1750 he made a late second marriage, which was dynastic. All the future dukes of Saxe-Meiningen were descended from this marriage.

Georg II accepted that he had little political influence in the new Germany led by Prussia, and turned his energies instead into making his duchy a centre of culture. He had the highest artistic standards and pursued his goals with drive and determination, making all the decisions himself. The amazing performance level of his orchestra in their guest appearances in Berlin in 1882, led to the foundation of the Berlin Philharmonic Orchestra[10]. But the duke's greatest love was the theatre and he also took over direction of the Meiningen Court Theatre, building this into a world-class company that toured from 1874 to 1890 and was famous for its scenery, costumes, and realistic acting. It is claimed that the Royal Shakespeare Company was modelled on the Meiningen Court Theatre[11]. It is his work in the theatre that earned Georg the nickname in history of the *Theatre Duke*.

Georg II was born in 1826; he was the son of Duke Bernhard II (1800-1882). From a young man, Georg took a different view on politics to his father. Bernard II believed in the old order and supported Austria for the leadership of Germany. His son, who could see that the wind was now blowing in quite a different direction, served in the Prussian army and married a Prussian princess. This must have helped when, in 1866, Austria was defeated by Prussia in the Seven Weeks War and its influence in Germany came to an end. Saxe-Meiningen was occupied by Prussian troops but avoided the fate of other German states that had sided with Austria, and was not annexed. Instead Bismarck forced Bernhard II to abdicate in favour of his son. It led to great bitterness between father and son and a breach that was never healed[12].

In 1850, Georg married Princess Charlotte of Prussia, a niece of the Prussian king. Their marriage was a success, but she died in 1855 giving birth to their fourth child, a baby boy who lived only a day. His second marriage in 1858, to Princess Feodora of Hohenlohe-Langenburg, a niece of Queen Victoria (her mother was the queen's half-sister), did not turn out so well and the couple drifted apart. The verdict is that Feodora was incapable of sharing his cultural and artistic interests, and that Georg had not got over his first wife[13]. After the birth of their third son in 1865 (who lived for only a few days), Feodora mostly stayed away. When she died from scarlet fever in 1872, Georg was having an affair with the actress Ellen Franz who would become his third wife.

45. Georg II of Saxe-Meiningen and his third wife,
the retired actress Ellen Franz.

Ellen Franz (1839-1923) joined the Meiningen Court Theatre in 1867. When she married Georg in 1873 she was forced to give up her career as it was completely unacceptable for the duke's wife to be on the stage. It was a morganatic marriage and she never became the duchess of Saxe-Meiningen; instead on their wedding day her husband gave her the title of Freifrau (baroness) Helene von Heldburg. Their marriage caused a scandal – the German kaiser was appalled that the widower of a Prussian princess should be married to an actress, and Queen Victoria was deeply upset. She wrote to her daughter

You asked if I am not 'rather shocked' at that horrid George of Meiningen's marriage. I think it disgraceful and an outrage to the memory of the dear wife he so shamefully neglected for this very woman![14]

Things cannot have been easy for Helene – there were resignations at court over her marriage, the army refused to salute her, and her disgruntled father-in-law (deposed only a few years before) threatened to go over his son's head and appeal to his subjects. All of this made her new husband very angry. It must have been especially hard to be forced to give up her career and the exhibition at Elisabethenburg said this 'caused her to enter a deep personal crisis'[15]. She continued to be involved in the Court Theatre, as artistic director and acting coach, and shared in her husband's achievements. Her marriage was a happy one that lasted for over forty years until Georg II died in June 1914, not long before the start of World War I. He was the reigning duke of Saxe-Meiningen for forty-eight years.

The exhibition (called *Muse's Court between Weimar and Bayreuth*) occupied a suite of rooms in the schloss that were remodelled for

46. The Blue Corner Room at Elisabethenburg.

Helene von Heldburg in the late nineteenth century in historicist style (we might call it Victorian). I enjoyed the exhibition, but I preferred the décor from earlier in the century, particularly the delightfully pretty Blue Corner Room which is dedicated to Queen Adelaide of Great Britain. She was the only princess of Saxe-Meiningen ever to become a queen when she married the duke of Clarence, later William IV of Great Britain. Her room is light and airy with turquoise panelling, accentuated with gold paint. On the walls are large state portraits of Adelaide and her husband and in the window, looking out, stands Adelaide herself (a mannequin) wearing a copy of the dress from her portrait. Queen Adelaide was a very sympathetic character and there is more about her story at the next schloss.

The tradition of music at Elisabethenburg continues today. As well as the museum, government offices, state archives and a café, the schloss is home to a music school and concert hall.

Altenstein

The name of Schloss Altenstein means ancient (or old) stone. The schloss was the summer residence of the dukes of Saxe-Meiningen and is in a lovely location to the north of their capital on the edge of the Thuringian forest. On our way there we went through the wooded area where the sham attack took place that allowed Martin Luther to drop out of sight (see The Wartburg). We arrived to find that Altenstein is not open to the public – it is under restoration and shrouded with scaffolding. But the gardens are open and well worth a visit. They are beautifully maintained, with tremendous views over the Thuringian countryside. And at Altenstein we had the adventure of being filmed as part of a programme for German television.

Altenstein was built in baroque style in the 1730s, for Duke Anton Ulrich of Saxe-Meiningen (1687-1763), but he never liked it. The story is that the official opening was a disaster when the duke realised his new schloss faced east, rather than south as he expected. He never

47. Altenstein is on the edge of the Thuringian forest.

went there again and the disgraced architect was forced to flee. It was only more than sixty years later (in 1798), during the reign of his son, Georg I (1761-1803), that Altenstein became a summer residence.

The schloss is a mile or so from the health resort of Bad Lieben-stein (Liebenstein means love stone), and this town owes its existence to Georg I. When staying at Altenstein, Georg I felt the benefit from drinking its natural spring water so, in 1800, he bought back land that had been mortgaged by his grandfather, laid a new road, and began to develop buildings to attract and accommodate visitors to his new spa. After Georg I died in 1803 his widow, Luise Eleonore of Hohenlohe-Langenburg, continued the development and built herself a home in the town called the Royal Villa, next door to the spa. Queen Adelaide, who was the daughter of Georg I and Luise Eleonore, returned from England several times to stay in Bad Liebenstein for her health. She was staying with her mother in the Royal Villa in 1819, to recover from the death of her first baby, when she received the news of the birth of the princess who would become Queen Victoria[16]. On a later visit, Adelaide's lady-in-waiting was given a tour of Altenstein and shown the queen's childhood bedroom. This is her description

... a bedroom with a common floor and not a scrap of carpet. On each side was a small bed with white calico curtains; two small tables for glasses, etc., and a few light chairs formed the whole of the furniture; and this bare and comfortless-looking room, at which many a fine English maid would turn up her nose, had been Queen Adelaide's and her sister's till they married[17].

Princess Adelheid of Saxe-Meiningen (Adelaide is the English form of Adelheid) was born in 1792. She was her parents' first child, after nearly ten years of marriage, and they must have despaired of having children. A glance at the Saxe-Meiningen family tree (see chart 9) shows how sons were sometimes thin on the ground. Adelaide's grandfather, Duke Anton Ulrich, was seventy-three years old when her father, Georg I, was born. Georg and his wife would wait another eight years after Adelaide for the birth of their only son, Bernhard II.

Adelaide was twenty-five years old when she received an offer of marriage from William, duke of Clarence, the third son of George III. Princesses were more often married in their teens and Adelaide may have thought she would be a spinster. Her sister Ida, who was younger,

48. King William IV of Great Britain and his consort Queen Adelaide.

had married sometime before. William had not met Adelaide and there was no romance at all involved in his offer. He had already made unsuccessful proposals elsewhere, and his main concern was to try to squeeze money out of the British Parliament. At one point it looked as if he would walk away from the engagement because they wouldn't stump up enough[18]. Nor was he a particularly attractive proposition personally – William was middle-aged (fifty-two), badly educated, and with a head which was described as having the shape of a pineapple[19]. He had rough manners, formed during his service in the Royal Navy which he joined at thirteen, and he drank and swore too much. His antics and behaviour had earned him the nickname of a *Silly Billy*. He also had ten illegitimate children at home.

Adelaide was a kind and gentle personality, but she wasn't a push-over. She had received a good education and also had role models in her mother and grandmother, each of whom ruled Saxe-Meiningen as regent for their minor sons. Adelaide's father died when she was eleven and her brother, who became Duke Bernhard II, only three. She decided to accept William's offer in the interests of Saxe-Meiningen and to provide her brother with a close connection to the powerful British throne[20]. Neither of William's two elder brothers had an heir, so there was a chance that William might become king. William did become king in 1830, after the death of his eldest brother, George IV.

William and Adelaide were married in July 1818. Their story has been compared to the fairy tale *Beauty and the Beast*, because Adelaide had such a positive influence on her husband. His manners improved and he became more considerate[21]. Their marriage was a success but, sadly, their babies did not survive. William's mistress, Mrs Dorothea Jordan, had previously given him ten children with little difficulty, but Adelaide's experience of pregnancy was very different. Their first baby, a daughter, was born prematurely on 29 March 1819, baptised Charlotte, and died later the same day. Another pregnancy ended in miscarriage in September that year. A second daughter, called Elizabeth, was born six weeks prematurely on 10 December 1820.

She would have been queen of England instead of Queen Victoria had she lived, but she died in agony from convulsions on 4 March 1821. The following year Adelaide miscarried twins and William wrote to his brother, the king, that he couldn't find the words

...to express my feelings at these repeated misfortunes to this beloved and superior woman...I am quite broken-hearted[22].

There may have been other pregnancies, but there were no more babies. When Adelaide died, she left a cherished possession to her niece by marriage, Queen Victoria – a statue of her little daughter Elizabeth sleeping on a couch.

49. The elegant Palais Weimar, where Queen Adelaide stayed on her visits to Bad Liebenstein.

Adelaide's brother, Bernhard II, always intended to make building alterations at Altenstein and various plans were drawn up, but none of them was ever implemented. After his abdication in 1866 Bernhard stayed on in the schloss until his death in 1882, and then his widow until she died in 1887. But when their dynamic son, Georg II, got his hands on the schloss things moved fast. In the two years between 1888 and 1890 Altenstein was transformed – from an eighteenth-century baroque palace into a late nineteenth-century version of an English country house. Looking at the pictures of the schloss before and after this remodelling, it's hard to believe it is the same building. Because of the furore over their marriage, Georg II and his third wife, the retired actress Ellen Franz, retreated from the royal scene. They found their friends, who included the composer Johannes Brahms, in the world of music and theatre and entertained them at Altenstein[23].

The Saxe-Meiningen family retained the ownership of Altenstein until 1941 when it was sold to the state government of Thuringia. Over the next forty years it was used as a barracks, then a workers' recreation home, and then for a forestry school. But on 4 February 1982, the schloss was destroyed in a fire caused by an electrical defect. The inside was completely burned out and the roof fell in. Since then restoration has been slowly underway and is due to be completed in 2017, when Schloss Altenstein will open to the public as a Johannes Brahms museum.

Our television adventure happened by chance when a film crew turned up as we were taking photos on the large lawn in front of the schloss. My husband is naturally gregarious and soon found out they were making a programme for a local TV series on Thuringian schlösser. We were invited to take part, and spent the next hour following the director's instructions and being filmed in different parts of the garden. We had to climb the steep steps to the tiny Ritterkapelle (Knight's Chapel) which is perched precariously on top of a great chunk of rock; gaze out over the knot garden into the Thuringian forest; and walk down a path towards the schloss, stopping at a particular point to look up at the roof! As part of the crew we were allowed up close to the schloss, inside the safety barriers where visitors to the gardens are not allowed to go. It was all an experience and when the programme was shown on the following evening – there we were, including a clip of my interview, dubbed into German!

At Altenstein we were welcomed by a courteous and helpful gentleman who was manning the information office. This was located in a supplementary building at the entrance to the schloss called the Hofmarschallamt (I am not sure how to translate this – something like the offices of the marshal, or senior officer, of the court). We also had a warm welcome in the tourist information office in the Palais Weimar in Bad Liebenstein. This elegant building is the Royal Villa, built in classical style between 1803 and 1806 by Queen Adelaide's mother. It was later renamed after Adelaide's sister Ida (the next owner) who was married to Duke Karl Bernhard of Saxe-Weimar-Eisenach. Today the Palais Weimar is the town library, but on the first floor, underneath the central dome, a grand room called the Kuppelsaal (domed hall) survives.

Wilhelmsburg

Schloss Wilhelmsburg in the town of Schmalkalden was built between 1585 and 1590 by Landgrave Wilhelm IV of Hesse-Kassel. Wilhelm (William) was a popular name in his family. There would be another eleven rulers before Hesse-Kassel was annexed by Prussia in 1866, and seven of them were called Wilhelm, and another Friedrich Wilhelm. They liked to give their first name to their schlösser and Wilhelmsburg (or William's Castle) is the first of three included in this book. (For Wilhelmsthal and Wilhelmshöhe, built by Wilhelm VIII and IX respectively, please see chapter six.) The great charm of Wilhelmsburg is that it was never remodelled in a later style and remains a wonderful example of renaissance castle architecture.

Wilhelm IV was a descendant of St Elisabeth through her daughter Sophie, who married the duke of Brabant (see the Wartburg). Wilhelm was the son of Landgrave Philipp der Grossmütige of Hesse. His epithet, which means *the Magnanimous*, shows that Philipp has enjoyed a good reputation in history. A very old book about the House of Hesse-Kassel, printed in 1740, called him

50. View of Schloss Wilhelmsburg and the terraced garden.

...one of the greatest Men in History; a Prince of such Valour and Wisdom, that notwithstanding Emperor [Karl V] was his Enemy, he had the greatest Sway of any Prince in the Empire.[24]

Philipp did however blot his copybook when it became known that he had secretly contracted a second, and bigamous, marriage. The revelation came at a particularly bad time when he was leading a group of princes in opposition to the Holy Roman emperor's religious policies. Philipp had to go cap-in-hand to the emperor for a pardon and this weakened his position. A special exhibition at Wilhelmsburg called *Fatal Lust –Philipp of Hesse and his Bigamy* (which opened after our visit), is about Philipp's relationship with his second, unofficial, wife, Margarethe von der Saale.

When Philipp died in 1567, Hesse was divided between his four sons from his official marriage to Christina of Saxony, and Wilhelm IV became the first landgrave of Hesse-Kassel. The other three sons got Hesse-Marburg, Hesse-Rheinfels, and Hesse-Darmstadt. Wilhelm's new state was named after his capital city of Kassel, but his inheritance also included a part share of the old castle at Schmalkalden. By an arrangement dating back to 1360, Schmalkalden was owned equally by the landgraves of Hesse and the counts von Henneberg. When the last count in the Henneberg line died in 1583, Wilhelm got sole ownership and was soon making building plans. Demolition of the old castle began in 1584 and the foundation stone for his new schloss was laid in 1585. Wilhelmsburg was officially completed with the consecration of the chapel on 23 May 1590[25].

The schloss is a square-shaped building, with four wings enclosing an internal courtyard. The front faces west but we approached from the south side, climbing the long flights of stone steps that traverse the terraced garden. There is a good view of the schloss from the bottom

of this garden (see illustration 50) and another good view, this time of the town, from the top terrace. More steps up a spiral staircase, in the corner of the courtyard, lead to the museum.

There was nothing in English at Wilhelmsburg (no English audio-guide, guidebook or handout), but we still had a good visit. What is so special about this schloss is the renaissance-style interior decoration. I had not seen this anywhere else before. Giant soldiers wearing period costume stand guard beside the doors, with spears at the ready – these are figures painted on the wall around the door frames. Other doorways are decorated with

51. Gateway in the internal courtyard at Wilhelmsburg.

painted shields and what looked like enormous, stylised, locks. And two rooms in the museum are especially memorable – the chapel and the White Hall.

The chapel at Wilhelmsburg is an important example of a preserved Protestant church from the end of the sixteenth century. In 1873 one admirer said 'In the whole of German Renaissance I know no interior of similar fineness of decoration'[26]. It is a dazzling space, decorated in white and gold, with three levels of windows around the room. We entered the chapel – much to my surprise – through a door onto the higher of its two galleries. We were very high up, close to the ceiling, and it made me dizzy to look over the balustrade at the floor far below.

The chapel is organised vertically on three levels with the pulpit on the middle level, reflecting the central importance of the sermon in a Protestant church service. The altar is on the ground floor, combined with a baptismal font set into the centre. Above it is the pulpit protruding from the first gallery, and facing the landgrave's box at the other end of the chapel. And above the pulpit, on the top gallery, is the renaissance organ. Amazingly this instrument, which is still in use, is the one commissioned by Wilhelm IV and played at the consecration service on 23 May 1590[27]. The decor in this renaissance chapel is simpler than churches in the later, more elaborate, baroque style. But there is a powerful feeling in the room and I could easily imagine a preacher thundering from the pulpit.

The White Hall (Weisser Saal) is next door to the chapel and where the household gathered before attending the service. It has no furniture and is quite bare, with plain wooden floorboards and white coloured walls. But the walls and ceiling are covered with beautiful plasterwork on which lots of small details have been delicately painted in grey, green, and gold. I could see flowers and garlands, animals, insects, scrolls and flourishes, even a few Latin words. And on either side of the two doorframes are elongated human figures with painted faces. In place of the tapestries which once hung on the side walls, there are now two large, impressionistic, canvas paintings. They fit in very well, and their colours (mainly tones of grey) complement the room. The curator told us the White Hall is always popular with visitors, who frequently ask for a postcard of it. I asked too – but they don't stock one in the shop!

52. Portrait of Landgrave Philipp the Magnanimous of Hesse.

During the Reformation, the town of Schmalkalden gave its name to both a group of Protestant princes and a religious war, and the museum at Wilhelmsburg tells the story of these events. In 1531 there was a meeting of Protestant territories from the Holy Roman Empire in the town, and a military alliance called the *Schmalkaldic League* was established, to defend their Lutheran religion against the Catholic emperor, Karl V. The league was led by Landgrave Philipp the Magnanimous of Hesse (see above) and Elector Johann Friedrich I of Saxony. For some years Karl V was distracted, by the threat of the Ottoman (Turkish) Empire in the east and of France in the west, and unable to deal with the League. But in 1547 he defeated it easily at the battle of Mühlberg, during the *Schmalkaldic Wars* (1546-1547). Both leaders of the League were taken prisoner.

Philipp was held for five years; despite what he thought was an agreement by the emperor to release him much earlier. But he did retain his lands. Johann Friedrich, on the other hand, was forced to sign over Saxony to a cousin from another branch of his family who had fought on the emperor's side. But the end of the League did not mean the end of the Protestant religion and many of the conquered territories refused to reconvert to Catholicism. The emperor was forced to give way and in 1555 the Peace of Augsburg endorsed the coexistence of the Catholic and Lutheran religions in the Holy Roman Empire and provided that '...neither Party should annoy one another under the Pretext of Religion'[28].

Wilhelmsburg was always a secondary residence for the Hesse-Kassel family and from the start of the nineteenth century was not used by them at all. For a century and a half the schloss endured as it was used for a hotchpotch of different purposes, including as a military hospital, offices, a youth hostel, allotments, and an institutional home. The turning point in its fortunes came during the GDR years, and in 1962 a continuous programme of renovation began. The restoration work included the White Hall, the chapel, and the renaissance organ. There was music in the schloss when we were there, and we paused to listen to a violin class in the Giants Hall, where a group of children were playing for their music teacher. Before we left the curator told us of a happy moment in the history of the schloss when, after German reunification, the head of the House of Hesse made a visit and she proudly showed him around.

6

HESSE AND
THE HOUSE OF HESSE

The federal state of Hesse stretches from the city of Kassel in the north to beyond Darmstadt in the south. The capital of Hesse is Wiesbaden and its largest city is Frankfurt, which is a major European financial centre. But in the time of the monarchy both Kassel and Darmstadt were capital cities themselves, of two royal states ruled by different branches of the House of Hesse. This chapter has schlösser from both of these – the electorate of Hesse-Kassel and the grand duchy of Hesse-Darmstadt. We shall see where Napoleon's brother partied; search for the site of a palace built by a British princess; and find out more about Prince Philip's family schloss.

We stayed in Schloss Hotel Kronberg near Frankfurt. Royal history enthusiasts will know this better as Friedrichshof (Frederick's House), the schloss built by the widowed Empress Friedrich of Germany as a memorial to her husband, Kaiser Friedrich III. The empress was Queen Victoria's eldest daughter (also called Victoria but always shortened to Vicky), and there is more about her story and about Friedrichshof in my first book. If you want to spoil yourself in luxury and steep yourself in royal history, Schloss Hotel Kronberg is a great place to stay.

Grand Ducal Schloss, Darmstadt

Princess Alice of Great Britain, the second daughter of Queen Victoria and Prince Albert, arrived in Darmstadt as a bride in July 1862. Her wedding to Prince Louis (Ludwig) of Hesse-Darmstadt on 1 July 1862 was overshadowed by the death of her father six months before, and described as 'more a funeral than a wedding'[1]. As the eldest daughter at home, a great burden had fallen on the shoulders of eighteen-year-old Alice. She helped to nurse her dying father and then took on the role of comforting her bereaved mother. Victoria's grief was intense and, years later, Alice still remembered those terrible first nights, when she lay next to her sobbing mother until they fell asleep from exhaustion in the early hours of the morning[2]. Louis feared his fiancé would back out of their engagement, but the wedding went ahead. Alice's marriage had been arranged by Prince Albert before he died and Albert's widow was determined to carry out his wishes.

53. Princess Alice as a young woman, before her marriage.

When Alice arrived in Darmstadt she found an enclave of her husband's family schlösser in the centre of the town. The Grand Ducal Schloss itself was the residence of the recently widowed Grand Duke Ludwig III of Hesse-Darmstadt, who was the uncle of her husband. This is where Alice's funeral would take place only sixteen years later, in the chapel of the schloss. Not far away on Wilhelminenstrasse, was the Prinz Karl Palais – the home of Prince and Princess

Karl, who were Alice's new parents-in-law. Prince Karl was the brother and also the heir of Grand Duke Ludwig, whose marriage had been childless. Alice's first home in Darmstadt would be a small house next door to her in-laws' schloss. And on Luisenplatz, in front of the Grand Ducal Schloss, was the Alexander Palais, home of another brother of the grand duke. Prince Alexander had made a non-dynastic marriage so that his wife and children were not entitled to his name or rank; instead they were given the name of Battenberg. Six years after Alice's death, her daughter would marry Prince Alexander's son. For a family tree of the grand duke and his brothers, please see chart 10.

Alice herself would also build a schloss in the royal enclave, called the Neues Palais, on Wilhelminenplatz. All of these central Darmstadt schlösser were destroyed as the result of a single night of bombing in World War II. *Brandnacht* (the night of fire) was on 11 September, 1944. After the war only the Grand Ducal Schloss was rebuilt and is there today. Where Alice's Neues Palais once stood is an open square called Georg-Büchner-Platz[3].

It was a pleasant surprise to emerge from the underground car park in Darmstadt and find ourselves standing next to an equestrian statue of Alice's husband, Louis. We had not been to Darmstadt before and driving around a big city in a foreign country can be stressful. So we just followed the signs for the centre of town (centrum), parked in the first convenient car park, and by luck found ourselves exactly where we wanted to be – in Ernst Ludwig's Platz, right in front of the Grand Ducal Schloss. But the schloss itself was rather a disappointment, because it looked so run-down and neglected.

The Grand Ducal Schloss at Darmstadt is a complex of different buildings, which grew up over more than six hundred years. It seems as if every ruler of Hesse-Darmstadt wanted to add to or change it. The oldest building is the Herrenbau (or Gentlemen's Building) and this originally dates back to the thirteenth century. The newest is a wing called the Neuschloss. This translates as New Palace, but I shall call it the New Wing to avoid confusion with Alice's Neues Palais.

The House of Hesse

The principality of Hesse was created in the thirteenth century when a younger son of the Duke of Brabant became Landgrave Henry I of Hesse. In 1567 there was a division of family lands between four brothers (see Wilhelmsburg in chapter 5). From this split, two lasting branches of the House were founded—the lines of Hesse-Kassel and Hesse-Darmstadt.

Wilhelm IV was the first landgrave of Hesse-Kassel, which was the senior of the lines. In 1803 Landgrave Wilhelm IX was elevated in rank and became Elector Wilhelm I. But a few years later, in 1807, his principality was expropriated and became part of the new kingdom of Westphalia ruled by Napoleon's brother, Jérôme. After it was restored in 1813, Wilhelm I continued to use the title of elector even though the Holy Roman Empire had been dissolved in 1806.

The last elector was his grandson, Friedrich Wilhelm I, who was on the losing side in the Seven Weeks War of 1866 and saw his principality annexed by Prussia. After his death in 1875 the succession passed to cousins, who reverted to using the title of landgrave.

Georg I became the first landgrave of Hesse-Darmstadt on the split in 1567. In 1806, Landgrave Ludwig X of Hesse-Darmstadt gained the more prestigious title of Grand Duke Ludwig I as part of the shake-up and reorganisation of states on the breakup of the Holy Roman Empire. This branch of the family was variously and at different times known as 'Hesse' and 'Hesse and by Rhine', as well as 'Hesse-Darmstadt'. For simplicity I have used only the latter throughout.

The last grand duke of Hesse-Darmstadt was Ernst Ludwig (always known as Ernie), whose mother was a daughter of Queen Victoria. He abdicated at the end of World War I, along with the other ruling German princes, and died in 1937. When his son Ludwig died childless in 1968, the line of Hesse-Darmstadt came to an end and the succession passed by family agreement to the senior Hesse-Kassel line. The two branches of the House of Hesse were reunited after four hundred years. The current head of house is Landgrave Donatus born in 1966.

The New Wing was built after a big fire badly damaged the schloss in 1715. The landgrave hoped to demolish all the buildings to make way for an entire new schloss, but shortage of money meant this could not be achieved. Only the New Wing was added and even then it was two hundred years before the interior was finally completed[4].

The New Wing is painted in pink and white and dominates the views of the Grand Ducal Schloss. I didn't find the New Wing a particularly attractive building and I preferred the older parts of the schloss. After World War II, these older buildings were so badly damaged that they had to be demolished and completely rebuilt; only with the New Wing was it possible to retain some of the original. The rebuilt schloss became part of the university but they recently moved out and it appeared to be empty when we were there, apart from the schloss museum in the Glockenbau (Bell Tower). The internal courtyards are used as a shortcut by the locals and I was shocked to see graffiti and peeling paint, with boarded up doors, broken dustbins, rubbish, metal barriers, and weeds everywhere.

54. The Neuschloss building dominates the view of the Grand Ducal Schloss at Darmstadt.

117

It must have been a culture shock for Alice when she arrived to live in Darmstadt. In the little house next door to her in-laws that was her first married home, the rooms were cramped and there was noise from the street[5]. It was a far cry from the comfort and privacy of her parents' homes, such as Osborne on the Isle of Wight with its en suite bathrooms! Alice built a new home for her family, called the Neues Palais, and made this as English as she could. When they moved into it in March 1866, she wrote to her mother that

...We are very comfortably established here, and I can't fancy that I am in Germany, the house and all its arrangements being so English. ..It reminds me a little of Osborne, of Buckingham Palace, a little even of Balmoral[6].

Alice used the dowry voted her by the British Parliament to build the schloss, but like so many other building projects, the Neues Palais ran over budget and strained her and Louis's financial resources. Alice's letters to her mother also complained that they had to borrow at Coutts Bank to help pay for the house, and couldn't afford to take a holiday[7].

55. Princess Alice built her own schloss called the Neues Palais.

The burial place of the Hesse-Darmstadt family – Rosenhöhe

There was one schloss in Darmstadt that was deliberately outside the family enclave. The marriage of Grand Duke Ludwig II and Grand Duchess Wilhelmine was not close and after the succession was secured by two sons, they lived a lot apart. Wilhelmine built her own summer residence on the edge of the town and called it Rosenhöhe, (Rose Hill or Heights). The schloss has since disappeared and Rosenhöhe is now a public park with the cemetery of the Hesse-Darmstadt family.

After her five-year-old daughter Elisabeth died in 1826, Wilhelmine built a mausoleum for her and began the tradition of Rosenhöhe as the family's burial place. Called the Old Mausoleum, this is an elegant building, in classical style, in a quiet part of the garden. Over the door is inscribed in Latin 'In Spem Aeterni Consortii', which roughly translates as 'In hope of eternal companionship'. This is where Princess Alice was buried, joining her two children who had died before her, Frittie and May.

At the beginning of the twentieth century Alice's son Ernie, the last grand duke, built the New Mausoleum for his parents and siblings. But when Ernie's own daughter Elisabeth died in 1903, aged eight, he buried her just outside the New Mausoleum, in the open air. On the headstone is a touching statue of a kneeling angel, protecting her grave with outspread wings.

Ernie died in 1937 and only weeks later tragedy struck when his eldest son, Georg Donatus, was killed in a plane crash together with his wife, his widowed mother, and his two young sons. They had been on their way to the wedding of Ernie's younger son, Ludwig, in London. Ludwig and his new wife adopted the baby daughter who had been left at home, but sadly she died of meningitis before she was three. The family are buried together in the garden at Rosenhöhe; together with Ludwig, the last of the line, who died in 1968 and his wife Margaret, who died in 1997. Their simple graves are well maintained and planted with flowers.

The cemetery is a short walk from the Lion Gate entrance to Rosenhöhe, which was also built by Ernie. The lions on the top of the pillars are affectionately known locally as sneezing hedgehogs!

Alice's life in Darmstadt was not completely happy. She became dissatisfied with her marriage, her relationship with her mother deteriorated, and she suffered a religious crisis. But worst of all was the death of a child in the Neues Palais. In May 1873, her younger son, two-year-old Friedrich Wilhelm (called Frittie in the family), was playing a

game with his elder brother when, by accident, he tumbled out of an open window. Frittie suffered from haemophilia and by evening he was dead from an internal haemorrhage. This genetic disease is transmitted down the female line and Frittie inherited the defective gene from his mother, Alice, who got it from her mother, Queen Victoria. One of Alice's brothers was a haemophiliac, so it was known to be in the family, but Frittie was the first sufferer in his generation. Only three months before his death he suffered a severe attack of bleeding, lasting several days, as a result of a small cut on his ear. Alice graphically described

56. Statue of Grand Duke Ludwig IV (Alice's husband) outside the schloss.

his suffering and the agonising medical treatment in her letters to her mother[8]. She never got over Frittie's death.

Alice died at the Neues Palais on 14 December 1878, aged thirty-five. This was the anniversary of her father's death seventeen years before. In early November her eldest daughter caught diphtheria and one by one most of the other children succumbed, and then her husband Louis. Alice nursed them all herself but on 16 November, four-year-old Marie (May) died. Alice herself is said to have caught the disease from comforting her son Ernst Ludwig (Ernie) over his little sister's death. I have an old commemorative print that depicts the moment of this embrace. Exhausted and at a low ebb, Alice was not strong enough to throw off the disease, and it proved fatal.

One of my goals for our visit to Darmstadt was to track down the site of Alice's Neues Palais. I had not been able to do this in my research before the trip, probably (with hindsight) due to confusion between the Neues Palais and the Neuschloss! As the schloss museum was closed (it was Monday) we asked in other likely places, including the State Museum, House of History, and the tourist information office. But no one had heard of Princess Alice's home. Eventually it was the curator in our next schloss who helped me track this down to the open square near the Grand Ducal Schloss called Georg-Büchner-Platz.

Jagdschloss Kranichstein

Shortly after Princess Alice arrived in Darmstadt in July 1862 as a new member of the family, Grand Duke Ludwig III took her to look at one of his schlösser as a possible summer residence. The grand duke owned about a dozen schlösser in and around Darmstadt and it was his habit to keep a small set of rooms in each of them and visit regularly, but only for a daytrip or to stay one night[9]. Alice was delighted with the schloss they visited and so Jagdschloss (Hunting Lodge) Kranichstein became her and Louis' summer home.

Today Kranichstein is just inside the Darmstadt city limits, about three miles north-east of the city centre. But in 1572, when it was bought as a hunting lodge by Georg I, the first landgrave of Hesse-Darmstadt, Kranichstein was more remote. Georg I remodelled the buildings, fenced in a game park, and planted a forest of pine trees. He also created a lake near the schloss, called the Backhausteich, and had the locals fulfil their labour service to him by digging it out by hand[10].

The schloss was in its heyday as a hunting lodge under landgraves Ernst Ludwig (succeeded 1678) and his son Ludwig VIII (succeeded 1739). They were passionate huntsmen and adapted Kranichstein for the newly fashionable *par force* hunting. This type of hunting is where,

57. An old picture of Jagdschloss Kranichstein with the Backhausteich (lake).

rather than driving the game to a fixed point where the hunters are waiting, the hunters pursue their quarry on horseback, with packs of trained hounds. Extra accommodation was added to the schloss for hunting guests, their horses, and the dogs; and wide avenues cut through the forest, in a star shaped pattern, to provide better views for the hunt followers (spectators). But when the next landgrave, Ludwig IX (son of Ludwig VIII) succeeded in 1768, he put an end to all this focus on hunting and Kranichstein became a summer residence[11]. It had not been lived in for more than eighty years when Grand Duke Ludwig III offered it to Alice. (Don't be confused by the numbering – when Landgrave Ludwig X was promoted to grand duke, they started a new run of numbers and he became Grand Duke Ludwig I).

Kranichstein is a charming place. The schloss is horse-shoe shaped, with three wings of uneven length. There is no view of the schloss from the car park and it was not until we turned the corner round the long left wing that it came into sight. Then what a nice surprise – above the centre of the main wing is a most unusual and decorative gable, painted in apricot colour with ivory flourishes, like icing on a wedding cake. The gable reaches high above the roofline, with curls and swirls along the edges, and decorative features on the flat face, including a clock, a sundial, and the family shield. On the very top, at the point of the gable, is the symbol of the schloss – a glittering sculpture of a crane, or kranich. This beautiful architectural feature was set off to perfection by a line of sweet chestnut trees planted down each side wing. These were in flower and their pink blossom framed the front of the schloss.

Alice and Louis moved into Kranichstein in June 1863 and spent a happy summer there. Her letters to her mother talk about bathing in the Backhausteich, and hearing her baby daughter 'shrieking' in the garden[12]. The couple's first child, called Victoria Alberta after both Alice's parents, had been born at Windsor Castle in April during a lengthy stay in Britain. Queen Victoria was not at all understanding about her new son-in-law's responsibilities as a future grand duke of Hesse-Darmstadt and the first years of Alice's married life were blighted by her mother's constant demands for lengthy visits home to Britain. But that summer of 1863 there were excursions around the area to meet relatives and neighbours, and they were able to entertain at Kranichstein where there was so much more room than in their small house in Darmstadt. Emperor Franz Josef of Austria came to Kranichstein in August, and in September there was a momentous event, when Queen Victoria visited. The queen wrote in her journal

It is a curious old house with gable ends, built round 3 sides of a court, with a pond near it. It is very comfortable inside and has many long corridors, full of magnificent stag horns. How these would have interested dearest Albert, as well as the curious old family pictures[13].

I was also struck by the long wide corridors at Kranichstein. The Grosser Hirschgang and Kleiner Hirschgang (the Big and Little Deer, or stag, Corridors) run around two wings of the schloss, connecting the historic rooms that are part of the museum tour. The walls of these corridors are lined on both sides with mounted stags heads and antlers (trophies of ancient hunts from centuries ago) and underneath are dozens of old pictures of hunts and hunting lodges. I also liked the Rondellsaal, described by Queen Victoria as 'a curious little room in a turret', where they had breakfast during her visit[14].

After Alice's death, Kranichstein was used less by her family. In 1917 her son, Ernie, had all his hunting equipment brought together at the schloss and opened a museum of hunting. Today the museum occupies two wings of Kranichstein, and the third wing houses a hotel, with a restaurant in the cavalier house. The ground floor of the museum houses the exhibition about the history of hunting and upstairs are the family rooms and the stag corridors. I am not in favour of hunting, and have never wanted to participate in any blood sport, but the contents of the hunting museum are interesting and have historic value. The young curator was very welcoming and, while we looked around, kindly researched and solved the mystery for me of the location of the site of the Neues Palais in Darmstadt!

58. The front of Kranichstein, with the decorative gable and sweet chestnut trees.

Alice and Louis had seven children – for a list of these, see chart 11. One of the first books I bought when I became interested in royal history was *Hessian Tapestry* by David Duff. This tells the story of Alice, her children, and grand-children, and is as dramatic as any thriller novel or television soap opera. Haemophilia stalked the family and Alice's daughters took it into the Russian and Prussian royal families. Two of her daughters, with five grandchildren, were murdered by Bolsheviks in the Russian revolution. One grandson and his family were wiped out in a plane crash in 1937, and another (Earl Mountbatten of Burma) was murdered, with other members of his family, on a fishing trip in 1979, when their boat was blown up by terrorists (the Irish Republican Army or IRA).

The playhouse at Wolfsgarten

Wolfsgarten is the private home of the Hesse family, but the gardens are open to the public for a short time each May to see the rhododendrons. As we were in the area on the right day, this was too good an opportunity to miss.

The playhouse in the garden built for Princess Elisabeth was absolutely delightful. Elisabeth was the only child of Ernie (the last reigning grand duke of Hesse-Darmstadt), by his first wife. Their marriage was unhappy and they divorced in 1901. Sadly little Elisabeth died of typhoid in 1903, when she was eight-years-old, while on a trip with her father to the tsar's hunting lodge in Poland (the tsarina was Ernie's sister).

Ernie built the single-story, two-roomed, playhouse for his daughter in 1902. It is a little girl's dream of a doll's house, painted blue and white, with a steep roof surmounted by a golden crown, a tall white chimney, and the initial E inside a large green garland on the gable front. Around the house is a small garden, enclosed by a picket fence. I loved the little golden dove on the top of each fence post.

Wolfsgarten was built in the 1720s as a hunting lodge by Landgrave Ernst Ludwig, who was mad about hunting. After his grandson gave up the sport it also, like Kranichstein, fell into disrepair until it was renovated as a summer residence by Grand Duke Ludwig III in the mid-nineteenth century. After Princess Alice died, her family used Wolfsgarten in preference to Kranichstein, and after he abdicated in 1918, Ernie made it the main family home. He had married for a second time in 1905 and his two sons from this second marriage, Georg Donatus (born in 1906) and Ludwig (1908) also played in the playhouse at Wolfsgarten.

Heiligenberg

At the top of the Heiligenberg (or Sacred Hill), nine miles south of Darmstadt, there is a small garden named the Cross Garden after the tall golden cross that stands in the middle. This glittering cross is made of cast iron gilded with gold, and is twenty-five foot high (nearly eight metres). It was put here by her children in memory of Grand Duchess Wilhelmine of Hesse-Darmstadt. There is a panoramic view of the Rhine valley from the garden, and it was one of Wilhelmine's favourite places. Later, her daughter-in-law, Princess Julie of Battenberg, liked to sit here too, and engage passers-by in conversation[15].

The two women never met, as Julie married Wilhelmine's son long after his mother was dead, but they were both unconventional for their time. Wilhelmine had a marriage of convenience and it was rumoured that a lover was the father of her three youngest children. Julie's marriage was morganatic, so that her children had no dynastic rights. Yet the descendants of these two relationships would sit on the thrones of Russia, Bulgaria, Spain, and Sweden. The Cross Garden is at Schloss Heiligenberg, a much-loved home of the Battenberg family.

Heiligenberg is on the outskirts of the village of Jugenheim. Today this is a quiet place and a far cry from the days when it was a bustling imperial summer residence and the tsar of Russia governed his vast empire from here. In the 1860s and 1870s the tsar and his family were regular summer visitors to the schloss, and the village would be jam-packed with their suite. During the so-called *Russian Years*, Schloss Heiligenberg played host to emperors and kings, and smart villas and guest houses sprang up in the village to accommodate their ministers and officials. In 1875 there was a summit meeting of the *Dreikaiserbund* (Three Emperor's League) at the schloss, attended by Kaiser Wilhelm I of Germany, Tsar Alexander II of Russia, Archduke Albrecht of Austria, and German Chancellor Otto von Bismarck[16]. The tsar was married to a princess of Hesse-Darmstadt, so their visits were family gatherings and reunions too. The grand duke of Hesse-Darmstadt (the tsarina's brother) had a schloss at nearby Seeheim, and Darmstadt and Kranichstein are not far away. Driven by all the royal comings and goings, Jugenheim became a thriving tourist destination.

But although we drove round and round the village, and knew it must be somewhere close, we could not find Heiligenberg. It was only after asking a local resident, who had lived in Jugenheim all his life, that we were put on the right track. Even then we nearly missed the narrow entrance with a discreet sign on the gates. Then it was up through the trees on a steep, winding drive, one kilometre long, to arrive at the schloss. But what do we do now? Everything looks closed – there are no signs anywhere and no one about. They say that fortune favours the brave, so we wandered into the courtyard and tried a few doors. Good luck led us to Monika, who very kindly showed us around and opened up the museum especially for us.

Grand Duchess Wilhelmine bought the Heiligenberg estate in 1827, the year after her little daughter Elisabeth died (see the text box on Rosenhöhe). The house was no more than a farmhouse then,

59. Schloss Heiligenberg was the summer residence of the Battenberg family.

but over the next sixty years Wilhelmine and her son Alexander, who inherited it from her, made additions and improvements until it was a sixty-room schloss with two towers and four wings around an open courtyard. Heiligenberg was a summer residence and the courtyard was always the focus of life here. Wilhelmine's granddaughter wrote in her reminiscences about 'the smell of russia [Russian] leather' in the courtyard, with 'Cossacks and sentries, and Punch (the tsar's dog)'[17]. The courtyard is still a pleasant place with patterned paving and cobbles, trees for shade, palm trees in pots, and a gentle fountain in the centre.

Wilhelmine was born in 1788 as a princess of Baden. At the beginning of 1803, her name was being mentioned around the courts of Europe as a possible second wife for Napoleon Bonaparte, at the time first consul of France but soon to become emperor[18]. Napoleon's marriage to Josephine had proved childless and he was desperate for an heir. But Josephine was adept at manipulating the emotions of her husband and, this time at least, any plans for a divorce foundered on her tears and entreaties[19]. So, at fourteen, Wilhelmine of Baden was back on the royal marriage market and quickly became engaged to her cousin, the future Grand Duke Ludwig II of Hesse-Darmstadt (his father and Wilhelmine's mother were brother and sister). They were married the following year, before her sixteenth birthday.

It was an arranged marriage and not a love match. Ludwig, who has been described as shy and awkward, had previously tried unsuccessfully for years to marry any one of Wilhelmine's five older sisters[20]. The couple seem to have managed to stay on good terms but once she had fulfilled her dynastic obligations by providing two sons (an heir and a spare), born in 1806 and 1809, Wilhelmine began to retreat from court. At some point she met the man who was described at Heiligenberg as her life partner. Baron August Ludwig de Senarclens-Grancy was Swiss and an equerry at the Hesse-Darmstadt court. When Wilhelmine bought Heiligenberg, a house was bought for Senarclens-Grancy in Jugenheim village[21]. There has always been speculation that Senarclens-Grancy was the father of Wilhelmine's three younger children, and this is stated to be the case at Heiligenberg. Elisabeth (born in 1821), Alexander (born 1823), and Marie (1824) were born many years after Wilhelmine's two elder sons. But they were acknowledged by her husband and treated as prince and princesses of Hesse-Darmstadt, so it is hard to know for sure.

When Wilhelmine died in 1836, the two surviving younger children, Alexander and Marie, were only thirteen and twelve years old. In her will Wilhelmine directed that Senarclens-Grancy should supervise their education, so perhaps he had some say in their upbringing. He stayed on at the Hesse-Darmstadt court after Wilhelmine's death, and only a few months later married a maid of honour with whom he had a daughter[22]. That it was important there be no cloud over the children's parentage was shown three years later when Grand Duke Alexander, heir to the Russian throne and the future Tsar Alexander II, was touring Europe looking for a bride. He met fifteen-year-old Marie almost by accident, when she was allowed to join the grown-ups after dinner[23]. Her mixture of extreme youth, ethereal beauty, and vulnerability

60. The twenty-five foot high golden cross is a memorial to Grand Duchess Wilhelmine.

were irresistible, and Alexander fell in love. They were married in St Petersburg in 1841. The tsarina's Hessian family connections and childhood memories were why they returned so many summers to Heiligenberg. And the connection to Russia proved valuable to Hesse-Darmstadt – this, and the link to Britain through Alice's marriage, helped to protect the little state from the same fate as others on the losing side in the war of 1866, of being annexed by Prussia.

61. Wilhelmine's youngest child became Tsarina Marie Alexandrovna, wife of Tsar Alexander II of Russia.

We spent a wonderful afternoon at Schloss Heiligenberg. This was never a grand palace, but more of a friendly and comfortable country house. Monika was a knowledgeable and enthusiastic guide and extremely generous with her time, even though she had a busy schedule and we were not expected. We saw the Garden Room, that once hosted the meeting of the Three Emperors League and can now be hired for events; the Princesses House, a playhouse where the children of emperors and grand dukes once romped and now a venue for children's parties; and looked round the gardens with the little bathhouse, the terrace with original cast iron urns installed by Grand Duchess Wilhelmine, and a pergola dripping with flowering wisteria. We also saw the new museum in the Russian House.

The Russian House is a small building in the grounds that gets its name because it housed part of the tsar's suite when he stayed at Heiligenberg. It is now a museum that tells the story of Wilhelmine, her son Alexander, and his Battenberg descendants. This museum is small, and is not open every day, but the contents are very interesting and have clearly been put together by curators with a passion for their subject. And there is plenty of information in English.

When Marie went to St Petersburg in 1841 to marry the heir to the Russian throne, her brother Alexander went along too, to keep her company and to further his own career. He turned out to be a born soldier and proved his bravery as an officer in the Russian army. But he upset Marie's father-in-law, Tsar Nicholas I, by his amorous adventures. First he tried to marry the tsar's daughter, Grand Duchess Olga, but was turned down by Nicholas, who had other plans for her. Then Alexander refused a match arranged by the tsar with his niece, Grand Duchess Catherine Mikhailowna[24]. And finally he carried on a love affair with his sister's lady in waiting, Countess Julie von Hauke, and made her pregnant[25].

Alexander of Hesse-Darmstadt married Julie von Hauke in Breslau in Silesia (now part of Poland) in 1851. Julie was a ward of the tsar; her father had been killed in the Polish revolution of 1830, defending the tsar's brother Constantine, who was governor-general of Poland. She was intelligent, aristocratic, and well-connected, but she was not of equal royal birth. So the marriage was morganatic, which meant that Julie could not take her husband's rank or title, and their children had no dynastic rights. Instead Alexander's brother, Grand Duke Ludwig III, revived the previously extinct title of Battenberg for Julie and the children. There would be five children – a daughter born soon after her parents' marriage (it seems she was christened four months before her official date of birth)[26], and four handsome sons. The Battenberg boys did well in life, notwithstanding their morganatic birth, and two of Julie's granddaughters would become queens. (Please see chart 12 for a Battenberg family tree.)

The Battenberg/Mountbatten family name

Battenberg was the family name of the children of Prince Alexander of Hesse-Darmstadt and Countess Julie von Hauke. As Alexander's marriage was morganatic, his family were not entitled to his name and titles; instead his brother, the grand duke, made them princes and princesses of Battenberg. The eldest of the four Battenberg princes – Ludwig or Louis, born in 1854 – joined the British Royal Navy at fourteen. When World War I broke out he was First Sea Lord of the Admiralty (head of the British navy). As a German prince with close connections to the German navy, his position was untenable and he had to resign. Louis's wife and the wife of Prince Heinrich of Prussia were sisters. Heinrich was the kaiser's brother and commander of the German Baltic Fleet. Louis spent the rest of the war in retirement.

In 1917, at the height of anti-German public feeling and hysteria, George V changed the German family name of the British royal family (Saxe-Coburg-Gotha, from Prince Albert) to the very English sounding 'Windsor' (taken from Windsor castle near London). At the same time, at the request of the king, Louis anglicised his Battenberg family name by neatly reversing the two halves and translating 'berg' into 'Mount' or mountain. Louis also gave up his German titles and the king gave him an English title as the first marquess of Milford Haven.

The mother of Prince Philip, husband of Queen Elizabeth II, was Louis' elder daughter. She was already married, to Prince Andreas of Greece and Denmark, when the family name was changed in 1917, so never used Mountbatten. Nevertheless, when Philip became a naturalised British subject prior to his marriage in 1947, this is the name he took. It raised the question of whether the name of the British royal family would in future be Mountbatten, but this has remained as Windsor.

The tsar was furious with Alexander over the affair and dismissed him from the Russian army. His brother dared not have him in the Hessian army, for fear of further upsetting the tsar, so Alexander became a soldier of fortune. He served as a general in the Austrian army and, by the time he retired, had achieved the distinction of being decorated by four different countries for valour on the field of battle (Austria, Prussia, Hesse-Kassel, Russia)[27]. When Alexander retired in 1862, the family returned to Hesse-Darmstadt and spent their summers at Heiligenberg, where they were visited by his sister Marie and her family. The *Russian Years* had begun.

Towards the end of our visit to Heiligenberg we walked through the grounds to see the Cross Garden with Wilhelmine's golden cross, erected by her children in 1866. On the way we passed an old 'Zent' lime tree, where local courts were held in the open air up to the eighteenth century, and the remains of a nun's convent abandoned in 1412. Wilhelmine 'enhanced' these to create a romantic ruin with gothic windows and baptismal font. The Cross Garden is a tranquil place; Alexander and Julie are buried at the foot of the golden cross and there is a memorial chapel, built by Julie after her husband died in 1888.

The views from here are tremendous – on a clear day you can see to the other side of the Rhine. Because Prussian victory in the Franco-Prussian war of 1870 was so swift, we forget that this is not what people expected to happen at the time. Heiligenberg was not very far from the French border, and the family expected an invading army to come their way. Alexander's son remembered how his father turned all their horses loose in the woods, so that they could not be requisitioned by the French[28]. At Kranichstein nearby, Princess Alice wrote to her mother that she could not possibly leave, in case there should be panic when the French arrived[29].

Heiligenberg was inherited by Alexander and Julie's eldest son, Prince Ludwig (Louis) of Battenberg, who was a career

62. The children of grand dukes and emperors once played in the Princesses House.

officer in the British navy and married to Princess Alice's eldest daughter. After World War I, Louis, now the first marquess of Milford Haven, was in more straightened circumstances and in 1920 he sold the schloss. In the 1930s it was taken over by the state of Hesse, for failure by the new owners to pay their taxes, and after World War II it became part of a teacher training college. That's how it was being used when Prince Philip made his private visit in 2005 (see chapter 1). Philip is the great-grandson of Alexander and Julie.

When the college finally left in 2010, management of the schloss was taken over by a new foundation (the Stiftung Heiligenberg Jugenheim) and renovation for its new life began. Today Heiligenberg is an events venue and business centre – renting office space to small businesses in the information technology, marketing, and human resources sectors. The museum in the Russian house opened in 2014 and the latest project, the Princesses House, was completed in 2015. There is a Christmas market in the courtyard and music concerts in the summer. On our way out we stopped at the bottom of the steep drive to look at the road name – 'Louis Mountbatten Street', after Alexander and Julie's grandson (Earl Mountbatten of Burma).

Burg Friedberg

I wanted to come to Friedberg because I knew that Tsar Nicholas II and his family spent several weeks here in 1910. But I didn't expect to find a town with a rich imperial history of its own, or a schloss that is an entire walled village! There is no museum here – the mansion where the tsar stayed is a tax office and we did not get past the rather grumpy gentleman on the public enquiry counter. But I enjoyed exploring the town of Friedberg and its next-door schloss – called Burg Friedberg.

The small town of Friedberg is in the Taunus hills to the north of Frankfurt. Nowadays it is famous mainly as the place in Germany where Elvis Presley was posted during his stint in the US army. But hundreds of years ago, this was one of the largest and most prosperous towns in

Hesse, and rivalled Frankfurt in importance. Friedberg's wealth was founded on cloth production – Friedberger cloth was highly prized and exported all over Europe. In the thirteenth century (1252) the town became an Imperial Free City, which means it had self-governing rights and was represented in the diet of the Holy Roman Empire. An Imperial Free City was subject directly to the emperor himself, which often led to conflict with local lords and princes.

Burg Friedberg is just to the north of the town, at the end of the long main street called Kaiser Strasse. It covers an enormous site (39,000 square metres) and is a complete walled village with moat, watch-towers, streets, houses, church and mansion. The burg was a separate political entity from the town and was governed by a burggrave (a rank below graf or count). On the break-up of the Holy Roman Empire at the start of the nineteenth century, both town and burg became part of the duchy of Hesse-Darmstadt.

The site of the burg has been inhabited since prehistoric times – the Romans had a camp here and the original schloss dates back to

63. The burggrave's mansion in Burg Friedberg, about the time
Tsar Nicholas II and his family stayed here.

Emperor Friedrich I (Barbarossa) in the twelfth century. The buildings in the burg are from a jumble of dates, as new ones were added or old ones altered over the centuries. The most recent is a school, built in the 1960s on the site of an old Roman bathhouse. We entered by the southern gate, built around 1500, and walked down the central street to the northern gate at the other end, which is the oldest building (1350) on the site. This is a fifty-eight metres high tower called Adolfsturm (or Adolf's tower) after Graf Adolf of Nassau who was taken hostage here in a skirmish of 1347. He was released after payment of a ransom and the story goes that the money was used to build the tower.

The burggrave's mansion, where the tsar stayed, is located on the right hand side of the central street, half way between the gates. It

was built between 1604 and 1610 by Burggrave Johann Eberhard von Kronberg and his wife. The single-wing renaissance building has three high gables with decorative scrolls and horns. In front is a courtyard with a single cavalier house and a triumphal arch (see illustration 63). The interior of the mansion was almost completely destroyed in a 1990 fire, but the exterior walls have been restored to the original style. The quoin stones on the corners of the building, the window frames,

64. The southern entrance gate to Burg Friedberg, built around 1500.

and the decoration on the gables are painted in a dusky pink. The colour contrasts well with the cream walls and brick arch and the mansion looks very attractive.

When Burg Friedberg came into the ownership of the grand dukes of Hesse-Darmstadt, the burggrave's mansion became an occasional summer residence. Grand Duke Ludwig III made alterations between

1845 and 1858, to provide a set of rooms for himself[30]. The grand duke was famous for having a lot of schlösser and he liked to get round all of them regularly, even if only for a very brief visit. Grand Duke Ernie changed the layout again for a very important occasion in the history of the burg – the visit of Tsar Nicholas II and his family between 30 August and 24 October, 1910.

Like his grandfather, Alexander II, Nicholas had also married a Hessian princess. Tsarina Alexandra Feodorovna, who was Ernie's sister, was born Princess Alix of Hesse-Darmstadt. Ernie and Alix were children of Princess Alice (see chart 11) and survivors of the diphtheria epidemic at the Neues Palais in 1878 that killed their mother and little sister (see Grand Ducal Schloss, Darmstadt). Because of the close relationship between the Hesse-Darmstadt and Russian royal families, Nicholas (called Nicky in the family) had known Alix since she was a child. They became engaged at Ernie's wedding to his first wife in April 1894.

65. Ernie of Hesse-Darmstadt, his second wife and two young sons.

By 1910 Alix was a chronic invalid and the visit to Friedberg was on the advice of her doctor, so that she could have treatment at the nearby spa town of Nauheim (now called Bad Nauheim), famous for its salt springs and cures for heart disease. Historians have debated whether Alix did suffer from a weak heart, as she believed, or whether her ailments were psychosomatic, brought on by stress and anxiety over the illness of her only son, Alexis. Like her mother, Alix was a carrier of haemophilia; and Alexis, heir to the Russian empire, suffered from the bleeding disease.

In her book about Alexis's four sisters, author Helen Rappaport highlights the logistical nightmare and expense of hosting the tsar and his family on their visit to Friedberg with an entourage of one hundred and forty, including Cossack bodyguards and Okhrana (secret police) agents as well as the household[31]. In her reminiscences, Princess Marie of Battenberg describes a similar hustle and bustle on the arrival of Alexander II and his family at Heiligenberg forty-two years before (in August 1868). They came with carts piled with luggage, carriages full of servants, doctors, ladies in waiting, the Home Secretary, and Chief of Police[32]. Both men were a target for assassination in Russia, and enjoyed these holidays in their wives' country when they were off-duty. While Alix took the cure and was pushed round Nauheim in a wheelchair, Nicholas abandoned his usual military uniform for civilian dress and enjoyed himself with the family. As well as Ernie with his second wife (Eleonore of Solms-Hohensolms-Lich) and two small sons, there were visits from his and Alix's three sisters and their families. With picnics and excursions, tennis, bicycle rides and shopping, it must have been a golden autumn.

Wilhelmshöhe

Schloss Wilhelmshöhe, just outside the city of Kassel, was the summer residence of the second royal family in this chapter – the electors of Hesse-Kassel. When we set out on our drive to Kassel, we did not have Wilhelmshöhe on our list to visit. We were headed for another schloss (Karlsaue) in the centre of the city. But for some reason we must have had the wrong address and our Satnav took us to a tennis club. Now hopelessly lost, we were not sure what to do, until we happened to turn onto a three miles long arrow-straight street called Wilhelmshöher Allee, that runs from the centre of town out to the schloss. There was Wilhelmshöhe in the distance, and hanging above it on the hillside, almost suspended in mid-air, the massive Octagon monument with the statue of Hercules on the top! As we drove down the Allee we had a grandstand view until, when we were almost there, the road swerved suddenly to the right to skirt the schloss. The final part of the Allee, renamed Königschaussee (Kings Highway), is not open to traffic and in the days of the electors was reserved for only the royal family and guests[33].

The story of Wilhelmshöhe begins with Landgrave Karl of Hesse-Kassel (1654-1730). Inspired by his travels in Italy, Karl had the idea to astonish his fellow princes and create a water garden out of an entire wooded hillside. It was an enormous building challenge; great swathes had to be cut through the dense forest before they could even begin to mark out the plan and start the preparatory water-engineering work. On the crest of the hill, above a long cascade of water, Karl built an enormous garden structure, called the Octagon, taking a theme from Greek mythology to symbolise man taming nature – the victory of the Olympian gods in their battle with the giants.

66. View of Schloss Wilhelmshöhe and the Octagon monument from Wilhelmshöher Allee.

The Octagon was built on a huge scale: Mount Olympus (the home of the gods) sits on top of the Giants Castle from where the cascade, some two hundred and fifty metres long and ten metres wide, pours down the hillside. It was a stroke of genius to surmount the structure with a thirty-metre-high obelisk so that, visually, it appears as if the cascade continues upwards to the sky[34]. And on top of the obelisk is a nine-metre tall Hercules (the symbol of strength), copied from a famous statue in antiquity. There is room enough for eight people in the cudgel that he leans on[35]! From the schloss at the foot of the hill, the panorama up through the garden to the Octagon a mile away is just breath-taking! *Wilhelmshöhe Park* is another of Germany's World Heritage Sites.

Karl's great-grandson, Wilhelm IX (1743-1821) built the schloss at Wilhelmshöhe (see chart 13). After he became the landgrave in 1785, Wilhelm lost no time in replacing the small renaissance schloss that was there in Karl's day with a monumental new building in contemporary classical style. When it was complete (in 1798) he asked his subjects to suggest a name and it became Wilhelmshöhe, or William's Hill.

67. The central wing of Wilhelmshöhe, called the *Corps de Logis*, was destroyed in World War II and the central dome, as seen in this old picture, has not yet been rebuilt.

Wilhelm was the son of Landgrave Friedrich II and Princess Mary of Great Britain. His parents' marriage fell apart when he was a toddler and his father converted to Catholicism. He may have done so in the hope of being eligible as a candidate to become elector of the Palatine, which was a Catholic state[36]. The landgraves of Hesse-Kassel were rich (they made money by hiring out Hessian soldiers to fight as mercenaries for other countries), but they craved an increase in their rank. Generations of landgraves pursued the goal of an elector's crown – the highest rank in the Holy Roman Empire apart from the emperor himself. A history of the family from 1740 gives an account of their estates and revenues and makes the case both for an additional elector, and for this to be the landgrave of Hesse-Kassel[37].

Her husband's conversion was anathema to Mary and her English family – it was only thirty years since her grandfather (George I) had picked up the British throne largely because the family were Protestant, and not Catholic. Wilhelm and his younger brothers went with their mother when their parents split up and he lived most of his life before he became landgrave in Denmark (where they had relatives). He was the landgrave who finally achieved the family ambition when Hesse-Kassel was made an electorate in 1803 and he became Elector Wilhelm I. But it soon became a hollow title when the Holy Roman Empire was disbanded in 1806.

Wilhelm built a schloss with three wings – the *Corps de logis* in the centre, with the Chapel Wing to the north and the Weissenstein (or White Rock) Wing to the south. This was named after his great-grandfather's schloss and an even earlier monastery on the site. At first the wings were three separate buildings but Wilhelm's son, Elector Wilhelm II, joined them up with a curved Gallery on each side. This created the unusually-shaped building, like a croissant, that we see today. The *Corps de logis* was destroyed by bombs in World War II and the magnificent central dome, seen in old pictures such as illustration 67, has not yet been rebuilt, though it is still hoped to do so[38]. Fortunately the Weissenstein Wing, with the apartments of Elector Wilhelm I, survived intact.

Our guided tour of the historic rooms in the Weissenstein Wing rattled along at a very fast pace. In forty-five minutes we saw I don't know how many rooms over two floors. As the tour was in German, we were given a helpful handout in English, but we moved from room to room so quickly that I hardly had time to read it.

The Kingdom of Westphalia

When French Revolutionary troops occupied the left bank of the Rhine in 1794, it was the beginning of the end for the Holy Roman Empire. Napoleon had no time for the old order and described the empire as '...an old whore who has been violated by everyone for a long time[39]. The end came in 1806 when the emperor resigned and the French destroyed the Prussian army at the battles of Jena-Auerstadt. Napoleon was master of Germany and decided the destiny of its princes. Some German territories became part of France, others were puppet states. And in 1807 he established an entirely new Kingdom of Westphalia.

The new kingdom was about twenty-five thousand square miles with a population of around two and a half million. It was comprised mainly of what had been Hesse-Kassel, with parts of Hannover, Brunswick and Prussia. For a king for the new country, Napoleon turned to his younger brother Jérôme. This was not a great choice, as Jérôme did not have a track record and would prove to be more concerned with his comforts than his responsibilities. He established himself at Schloss Napoleonshöhe in Kassel with his second wife, Princess Catherina of Württemberg (Jérôme had abandoned his first, American, wife on the orders of his brother).

Napoleon wanted the new kingdom to be a model for other vassal states in his empire, and wrote his brother a letter of detailed instructions. Personal service (serfdom) was abolished, administration streamlined, and the legal code reformed. Westphalia was the first of any German state to have a written constitution. Napoleon's view was that when the citizens of the new country saw how well they were governed, they would be content.

But Westphalia paid heavy taxes to France and its men were conscripted into the French army. Unrest always simmered and there was open revolt in 1808. In 1813, after the disastrous retreat from Moscow had loosened Napoleon's hold, there was another revolt in favour of the deposed Wilhelm I. French troops reinstated Jérôme, but his reprieve was short. After the battle of Leipzig (October 1813), Napoleon withdrew to France, the kingdom of Westphalia collapsed, and the elector of Hesse-Kassel was restored.

The blinds were drawn to protect the period furnishings from the sun, but the schloss does have fantastic views. In the Red Gaming Room the guide briefly raised a blind so that we could better see the portraits of Wilhelm's maternal grandparents, George II and Queen Caroline of Great Britain. Out of the window was a wonderful vista across the Schloss Park to Kassel in the distance. I liked the Marble Bathroom, where Elector Wilhelm II installed a circular sunken marble bath, heated by a stove underneath, rather like a hot tub; and the semi-circular Apse rooms on each floor that join the Weissenstein Wing to the curved Gallery building. But my favourite, because of its associations, was the Jérôme Room.

Between 1807 and 1813 Elector Wilhelm I was exiled from his country and Hesse-Kassel was part of the new kingdom of Westphalia, with Napoleon's younger brother, Jérôme, as king. Wilhelmshöhe became Jérôme's residence and was renamed Napoleonshöhe. King Jérôme was a frivolous lightweight, who was known in Westphalia as *The Party King*. He only apparently knew only one phrase in German – 'Morgen Wieder Lustik' which literally translates as 'Tomorrow again fun'[40]. In his portrait in the Jérôme room, *The Party King* looks rather dwarfed by his regalia and ermine robes. When the French arrived in Kassel they found the schloss almost empty of contents as the Hesse-Kassel family had taken everything with them when they fled. The Jérôme room has some of the new Empire style furniture that Jérôme commissioned to replace it.

On the evening of 5 September 1870, another member of the Bonaparte family arrived at Wilhelmshöhe. After the surrender of his army at Sedan in the Franco-Prussian War and the collapse of the French Second Empire, Napoleon III spent six months in captivity at the schloss before he went into exile in England. On his first day there, Napoleon remembered that he had visited Wilhelmshöhe fifty-seven years before, in the time of King Jérôme, and said he wondered if there were any souvenirs of the past. Walking slowly through the rooms he suddenly stopped short – he had found a portrait of his mother[41]!

68. Emperor Napoleon III meets with Prussian Chancellor Bismarck in a
peasant's cottage after the French army surrender at Sedan;
he left from this meeting for captivity in Wilhelmshöhe.

Wilhelmsthal

Schloss Wilhelmsthal is at Calden, just six miles from Wilhelmshöhe along a forest lane. It wasn't on our list to visit, but after the guided tour at Wilhelmshöhe my husband and I got chatting to a curator. When we mentioned our intention to try to find the schloss in central Kassel, he urged us not to do this but to go to Wilhelmsthal instead. Everything is original and it's much more interesting, he said. We have learnt from experience that such recommendations are usually worthwhile, and so we followed his advice. Thank goodness we did, because this small schloss is a masterpiece of rococo art. I love the rococo style and so it was a great delight for me; Wilhelmsthal is another of my favourite schlösser in this book.

When we arrived, we were greeted by the putti, or gilded statues of chubby little boys. These cherubs used to gambol in a grotto in the park outside until severe damage meant they had to be rescued a few years ago and brought inside for storage[42]. The little figures, that are made of cast lead, had lost limbs and become cracked and deformed, due to the ravages of the weather and also vandalism. Now only a few are on display in the entrance hall as part of an appeal to raise funds for restoration. The name of the appeal inviting visitors to donate is *Godparents for Putti*.

Wilhelmsthal was built by Landgrave Wilhelm VIII of Hesse-Kassel, who was the son of Karl (who had created the water garden and Octagon monument) and grandfather of Wilhelm IX (who would later build Schloss Wilhelmshöhe). It is confusing that these two schlösser are called after their builders, who had the same name – Wilhelmshöhe translates as William's Hill and Wilhelmsthal as William's Valley. Wilhelm VIII chose a rural spot to build his new leisure palace and hunting lodge. Work started in 1747, but was disrupted by the Seven Years' War and not complete when Wilhelm VIII died in 1760; the schloss was eventually finished by his son, Friedrich II, in 1773. (See chart 13 for the builders of Wilhelmshöhe and Wilhelmsthal.)

69. Schloss Wilhelmsthal is a masterpiece of the rococo style.

Wilhelm VIII was a second son and as a young man forged a successful military career in the Netherlands. But his elder brother Friedrich (who was heir to Hesse-Kassel) married the heiress to the Swedish throne and became the king of that country when she abdicated her rights in his favour. So when their father died in 1730, Wilhelm was required to return to Hesse-Kassel and rule as governor for his brother. He became landgrave in 1751 after Friedrich died. His brother's marriage was childless so that Wilhelm had also been required to get married – at quite a late stage, when he was well into his thirties. The marriage was not a success; his wife was pockmarked from a childhood disease and became mentally ill and was locked away[43].

What is special about Wilhelmsthal is that much of what you see – both the layout of the rooms and the décor – is original from the time when it was built. The schloss has been restored (the last restoration was in 1961 and took twenty years) but has never been altered or badly damaged. What this means is that the visitor can get a real glimpse into the life of the landgraves in the eighteenth century, and of their servants too. As well as the rooms of the landgrave and his guests, the guided tour includes some of the servants' quarters. I was impressed with a handy little arrangement whereby a concealed door at the side of the bed in the landgravine's bedroom leads first to her private lavatory, then to a kitchenette where her maid could prepare hot drinks, and finally to a small room that doubled as the walk-in wardrobe of the mistress and bedroom of the maid. The kitchen occupies the right wing of the schloss and is also on the tour, with vast kitchen range and old-fashioned cooking utensils.

Wilhelm VIII employed the best architects and decorators for the design and furnishing of his new schloss, including François Cuvilliés (architect at the Bavarian court in Munich) and Johann August Nahl (who worked for Frederick the Great). The rococo style is characterised by elaborate but delicate decoration, and the use of curves, light colours, gold, and mirrors to create a feeling of elegance, lightness, and informality. At Wilhelmsthal we saw a series of gorgeous rooms in this playful style, decorated in pastel colours with elaborate plasterwork and gilding. This is a delightful place and a real contrast to the much more formal and imposing classical style at Wilhelmshöhe.

70. The garden front at Wilhelmsthal.

We started in the *Beauty Gallery* (Schönheitengalerie) on the ground floor; named after the twenty-eight portraits of beautiful women that line its duck-egg-blue walls. These were commissioned by Wilhelm VIII from Johann Heinrich Tischbein the Elder, who was court painter in Kassel and a famous portrait painter of the eighteenth century. There are sixty-four of his paintings in total at the schloss, making it the largest Tischbein collection in the world[44]. A gallery of beauties was not a new idea, but what is unusual about this one is that these ladies are from different walks of life, and not just from the aristocracy. They were all known personally to Wilhelm VIII and selected by him on the basis of their looks alone[45].

Upstairs the landgravine's bedroom is hung with beautiful turquoise watered silk from France. The bedspread and drapes on the four-poster bed are over two hundred years old![46] Next door the panelled walls of her music room are decorated with delicate carvings of musical instruments (such as lutes, harps and flutes), and little Meissen porcelain figures of musicians. Many of the rooms are small and intimate; the largest is the Dancing Hall (ballroom), painted in glowing peach with a sea-green cornice. Here the carvings on the wall panels represent the

147

71. The beautiful women in the portraits in the *Beauty Gallery* were all known personally to Landgrave Wilhelm VIII.

four seasons – carnival masks for winter, garden tools for spring, grain for summer, and grapes for the autumn. For me the absolute highlight was a room with lemon yellow walls called the Cabinet of Parrots. Here every surface (walls, doors, curtains, chair covers) was decorated with motifs of parrots and other exotic birds.

It always surprises me how, apart from some that are well-known, there are generally so few visitors at schlösser. At Wilhelmsthal it looked as if we would be the only people on the guided tour until, at the last minute, two German ladies turned up. This turned out to be a big plus as they spoke English and kindly helped with translation. One lady was an art historian and I was not surprised to hear that Wilhelmsthal is also a favourite schloss for her, where she has returned time and again.

7

RHINELAND-PALATINATE, THE NASSAU-DIEZ AND HOHENZOLLERN FAMILIES

The state of Rhineland-Palatinate (Rheinland-Pfalz in German) is famous for its vineyards and beautiful river valleys. The river Rhine flows through the state and is joined, near Koblenz, by the Mosel from the left bank and the Lahn from the right. The stretch of the Rhine from Bingen to Koblenz, where it runs through a steep gorge lined by schlösser on both banks, was one of Europe's earliest tourist destinations and is now a World Heritage Site (*The Rhine Gorge*).

Historically the state was a jigsaw of territories. For example, in 1700 the lands around the forty-mile stretch of the Rhine Gorge were split between seven different principalities – the ecclesiastical electorates of Cologne, Mainz, and Trier, and the secular states of Hesse-Darmstadt, Hesse-Kassel, Nassau, and the Palatinate[1]. When the Holy Roman Empire was disbanded there was a reorganisation of lands, and at the end of the Napoleonic Wars in 1816 there were four areas in what is today's federal state. These were Rhenish Prussia (part of the kingdom of Prussia), Rhenish Hesse (part of the grand duchy of Hesse-Darmstadt, the Palatinate (part of the kingdom of Bavaria), and the duchy of Nassau.

The scenery of the Rhine has always inspired artists, musicians, and poets. The young Goethe was one of the early tourists in 1774, and wrote of '...the tree-covered cliffs, the enthroned castles, and the blue ridges of mountains looming out of the distance'[2]. Longfellow and Byron wrote poetry to the river; Turner painted it in watercolour; and Wagner set his cycle of operas called *The Ring of the Nibelung* around the river and its legends. During our visit to Rhineland-Palatine we would discover how the gift of a Rhine schloss inspired a romantic king to rebuild it as a make-believe castle where he could escape into the past. We also learnt about the strange health regime of a British king, and joined up with Dutch tourists on the trail of the origins of their royal family.

Bathhouse Palace, Bad Ems

We stayed in Häcker's Grand Hotel in the spa town of Bad Ems on the river Lahn. The hotel occupies the historic Kurhaus (Spa House) building and has a spectacular location on the bank of the river. The history of the building is closely linked to that of the spa, and it was built three hundred years ago by the Nassau-Diez family as their Bathhouse Palace.

A spa town is a health resort with a mineral spa or spring whose waters have medicinal benefits. They have a long history and Bad Ems is one of the oldest – the Romans may have bathed in its warm waters. With the end of the Roman Empire of the West, the Roman bathing culture fell into oblivion in Europe; it was only rediscovered in the Crusades when knights and pilgrims came into contact with the higher standards of cleanliness and hygiene in the Orient. Bathing in natural hot springs was revived and the earliest record of a bathing place at Bad Ems dates from the 1320s. These early spas were known as

Wildbad, (wild baths) because they were usually in the countryside and not protected by town walls. This was not without its hazards – Graf Eberhardt von Württemberg was in his Wildbad in 1367 when he was attacked by marauders and barely escaped with his life[3].

As bathing in spa waters came into fashion with the nobility, hot springs became a lucrative source of income for their owners. The development of Bad Ems was a joint venture between the counts of Nassau and of Katzenelnbogen, who ruled the area jointly. In 1438 they entered into a joint venture agreement to each build their own ducal bathhouse adjoining the thermal springs, on roughly the site of the Kurhaus today. When the counts of Katzenelnbogen died out in 1479, the landgraves of Hesse inherited their share.

72. The Kurhaus at Bad Ems was built three hundred years ago
as the Nassau-Diez Bathhouse Palace.

Over the centuries the bathhouses and bathing facilities were extended and rebuilt as Bad Ems became a popular watering place for German dukes and princes. Landgrave Philipp of Hesse-Butzbach and his wife visited in the 1630s, accompanied by two carriages, thirty-

73. Strolling along the promenade outside the Kurhaus in 1840

eight horses, and an entourage of fifteen. Their daily regime included one to two hours immersed in the waters, as well as fishing, walking, and excursions. Duke Johann Friedrich of Brunswick-Lüneburg came with a huge retinue in 1679. He was accompanied by one hundred and twenty-five people and one hundred and thirty horses[4].

The popularity of the spa led to a building boom at the end of the seventeenth century and grand lodging houses sprang up around the ducal bathhouses. Imperial Field Marshal Hans Karl von Thüngen built the Vier Turme (Four Towers) schloss (also sometimes called the Karlsburg) just down the river bank; and the archbishop-elector of Mainz built his own bathhouse palace across the river, on land that was part of his territory. It was clear that the ducal bathhouses needed to be modernised and in 1695 the two families (now the landgraves of Hesse-Darmstadt and the counts of Nassau-Diez), entered into a further agreement about the terms of rebuilding. The landgraves were quick off the mark with their new bathhouse, but for various reasons (including death in the family and lack of funds) work on the Nassau-

Diez side was delayed. Their new Bathhouse Palace was built between 1711 and 1721 by Princess Henriette Amalie of Nassau-Diez. We shall come across her again at our next schloss.

The new Bathhouse Palace had a central *Corps de logis* and a connecting East Wing. The design and appearance of these are still visible in the present Kurhaus building. After Bad Ems became Prussian in 1866, the East Wing became the summer residence of Kaiser Wilhelm II, who came here for his holidays each year for twenty years (between 1867 and 1887). It was renamed the *Kaiserflügel* (Emperor's Wing) in his honour and still has that name today. Wilhelm left off his military uniform when he was on holiday in Bad Ems, and the only statue of him wearing civilian dress is in the Kurpark (Spa Park) near the hotel. Our room was the western side of the hotel, in the old Lahnbau (River Lahn building), which was on the Hesse-Darmstadt side of the spa complex. From our balcony we had a perfect view of the river valley and historic Bad Ems.

In the eighteenth and nineteenth centuries a galaxy of European royalty visited Bad Ems to take the cure. Margravine Wilhelmine of Bayreuth (the sister of Frederick the Great) came on the advice of her doctors in 1737, in a fruitless attempt to improve her fertility. She only had one child, a daughter born in 1732. Electress Maria Anna Sophie of Bavaria stayed in the Nassau-Diez Bathhouse Palace for the same reason thirty years later, in 1763, but also to no effect[5]. She was the wife of the last elector of the Wittelsbach old Bavarian line, Maximilian III Joseph, who died childless in 1777 (see Augustusburg in chapter 2 and chart 1). The portly duke of Clarence (soon to be King William IV of Great Britain) came in 1825, and spent two months in the Vier Turme schloss. His regime sounds drastic and rather strange – he drank nothing but sherry and never ate any vegetables! William took long walks and on rainy days did physical jerks instead, in front of an open window in the schloss[6]. Walking was always part of the mineral water cure and the Kurpark, which stretches from the river bank up to the top of the steep hillside, dates as far back as the seventeenth century.

The Benedetti stone

On the promenade outside the Kurhaus there is a roughhewn block of stone inscribed with the simple message '13 July 1870, 9 hours 10 minutes in the

morning'. This records the date, time, and location of the famous incident that triggered the 1870 Franco-Prussian War, known as The Bad Ems Telegram.

At ten minutes past nine on the morning of 13 July, King Wilhelm of Prussia was on his morning walk when he was approached by the French ambassador. On behalf of his government, Count Benedetti asked the king to guarantee that no

Count Benedetti accosts King Wilhelm.

member of the Hohenzollern family would be a candidate for the vacant throne of Spain. The king courteously declined and reported the incident by telegram to his chancellor, Bismarck, in Berlin. Bismarck saw his chance to goad France into declaring war. He edited the telegram, omitting the courtesies and making it appear that the Prussian king had insulted the French ambassador; he then released it to the press. The public temperature in both countries rose to fever pitch, and France declared war on 19 July.

Defeat was swift – on 2 September the French army surrendered and Emperor Napoleon III was taken into captivity at Wilhelmshöhe (see chapter six). This victory over France, the traditional enemy of Germany, generated the national enthusiasm and pride that led to King Wilhelm being acclaimed as kaiser (or emperor) of a new German empire by the other ruling German princes, in the Hall of Mirrors at Versailles Palace near Paris in 1871. He became Kaiser Wilhelm I.

A long line of small metal plaques set in the pavement outside the Marble Hall (the centre of social life in Bad Ems) records the names of royalty and other celebrities who visited in the nineteenth century. They include – to name only a handful – King Friedrich Wilhelm IV of Prussia (1819 and 1825), King Ludwig I of Bavaria (1840), the famous singer Jenny Lind, known as the Swedish Nightingale (between 1849 and 1855), King Karl I of Württemberg (1875 and 1876), and the composer Richard Wagner (1877). All three of the German kaisers who reigned in 1888 (known as *The Year of the Three Kaisers*) visited Bad Ems the year before – Wilhelm I, Friedrich III, and Wilhelm II.

Tsar Alexander II of Russia made his first visits to Bad Ems in 1838 and 1840, before he came to the throne. There was then a gap of thirty years before he came again – this time for several years in the 1870s, when he arrived in May or June and stayed for four to six weeks. Alexander travelled under the alias of Graf Borodinski, but seems to have made no attempt to conceal his identity. The town was decorated and illuminated for his arrival, crowds turned out at the station to greet him, and the band played the Russian National Anthem. For the initial visit in 1870 the Town

74. Tsar Alexander II stayed in the Vier Turme schloss.

Council decided to spend nearly two percent of their annual budget on the arrival celebrations[7]. Alexander and his suite occupied the whole of the Vier Turme that was rented under a detailed contract with the hotelier. The schloss had to be decorated prior to the tsar's arrival and one room furnished as a kennel for his Newfoundland dog[8]!

75. The fascinating museum at Bad Ems about
the history of the spa and its royal visitors.

I found many fascinating details about these royal stays in a small museum about the history of Bad Ems, which is in the old Town Hall, not far from the Vier Turme. Although there was no translation into English, I had a wonderful time looking at the exhibits. On display was a hand-written account book for Crown Prince Friedrich of Prussia's stay in the Vier Turme between 13 April and 14 May 1887; also the printed spa guest list for 24 June 1871, showing Graf and Grafin Borodinski (the tsar and tsarina) staying at the Vier Turme, with their children Marie, Serge, and Paul. The spa guest lists also show that the tsar's long-term mistress, Katharina Dolgoruki, was often staying in Bad Ems at the time of his visits. She usually travelled using the name of her maid (Vera Borodikova), and is registered under that name at a villa just across the river from the Vier Turme during the entire time of the tsar's stay in 1874[9].

In the museum there was an old film showing Bad Ems in the summer of 1914. The town has never recovered the prosperity it enjoyed as a health resort prior to World War I. After the war the number of wealthy visitors dropped, and since World War II most of the guests taking the cure in Bad Ems have been sent by social insurance companies. With cuts in social benefits, their numbers too have dried up.

Bad Ems is a town for strolling and the main sites of historical interest are within easy walking distance. Our walking route took us along the Promenade, past the Marble Hall, Spa Theatre and Casino, then through the Kurpark to the Vier Turme and the Bad Ems museum. Coming back we meandered along the long street called Römerstrasse, which is lined with grand hotels built to accommodate guests in the spa's heyday. The names of these buildings are resonant of the rich and famous international set that came to Bad Ems – Haus Nassau, Herzog von Leuchtenberg, Russischer Hof, Englische Hof...

Oranienstein

Schloss Oranienstein provided some surprises. To start with, it was a surprise to arrive and find ourselves outside the locked gates of an army base. The schloss was occupied by French troops after World War II and when they moved out the state of Rhineland-Palatinate could not afford the costs of repair. The Federal government stepped in and renovated Oranienstein; and in May 1962 it was taken over by the Bundeswehr (German armed forces) as the headquarters of the Fifth Panzer Division. Today it houses the Army Regional Medical Care Command and they share it with a museum.

The military guard on duty told us there would be a tour of the museum later in the morning, but until it began we must wait outside the gates of the base. A small group gathered until, right on time, the tour guide turned up and the guard unlocked the gate. The guide then escorted us through the base, past military signs (such as 'no entry for tanks'), the entrance to an old underground shelter, and several buildings. Around a corner and the baroque schloss suddenly came into sight – looking elegant and gracious, with grey curving roofs and yellow walls with the decorative details picked out in white.

Another surprise was that most of the other visitors on our tour were Dutch. They were following a tourist trail called *The Orange Route*, which runs from Amsterdam in the Netherlands through ten federal states of Germany, connecting sites that are linked to the history of the Dutch royal family. The Dutch visitors explained to us that King Willem-Alexander of the Netherlands is descended from the builders of Oranienstein, and that the schloss is one of the four so-called *Mother Houses* of the House of Orange (the name of the Dutch royal family).

76. Schloss Oranienstein was built by Princess Albertine Agnes of Nassau-Diez; she named it in honour of her Dutch heritage.

Oranienstein was built between 1671 and 1684 by Princess Albertine Agnes of Nassau-Diez, the nine times great-grandmother of King Willem-Alexander. When her husband died in 1664, Albertine Agnes was assigned the old schloss in the nearby town of Diez as her dower house. She did not regard this old-fashioned schloss as grand enough for her station in life, and so built a new one instead, on the site of a former monastery just outside the town[10]. She was born a princess of Orange from the Netherlands and she called the schloss Oranienstein (orange stone) in honour of her Dutch heritage.

Albertine Agnes was the second of four daughters of Friedrich Heinrich, prince of Orange and stadtholder of the United Provinces of the Netherlands (stadtholder was a peculiarly Dutch rank and the closest thing to a king in the Dutch Republic). All the four daughters married German princes and they all built schlösser in Germany with Orange in the name. There is a reproduction at Oranienstein of a sumptuous portrait of the four sisters, by Jan Mijtens, in which they recline in an idealised landscape, dressed in silks and satins. The original painting was part of the *Orange inheritance* of Henriette Catharina (the third sister) when she married the prince of Anhalt-Dessau, and we had already seen this picture at Mosigkau (see chapter four). Chart 14 in appendix D shows the four princesses of Orange and their schlösser – the other three are Oranienburg in Brandenburg, Oranienbaum in Saxony-Anhalt (see chapter four), and Oranienhof, which was in Bad Kreuznach in Rhineland-Palatinate but is now destroyed.

Albertine Agnes's son married Henriette Catharina's daughter, and their joint grandson became the prince of Orange, and the ancestor of future Dutch kings and queens, when King William III of England died in 1702. William had no children and was succeeded in England by his deceased wife's sister, Queen Anne. But he was also prince of Orange and stadtholder of the Netherlands and he bequeathed this inheritance to his cousin, Johann Willem Friso of Nassau-Diez. The bequest was contested by King Friedrich I in Prussia (another cousin of William III) and the matter wasn't settled when Johann

77. The stunning *Cour D'Honneur* at Oranienstein.

Willem Friso drowned in Holland in 1711, on his way to a meeting in The Hague to negotiate the dispute[11]. He and his party were being

78. The colours in the elegant Blue and Gold Salon are from
the crest of the Dutch royal family.

ferried across a river when a gust of wind overturned the boat.
Everyone was saved, except Johann Willem Friso and his Master of
Horse. The prince stayed sitting in his carriage during the crossing
to shelter from the rain[12]. He was twenty-three years old. Chart 15
shows the relationship between William III and Johann Willem
Friso and how the latter became the founder of the Dutch royal line.

Six weeks after his death, Johann Willem Friso's son was born –
the new prince of Orange, Willem IV. The family tree of the counts of
Nassau-Diez shows a pattern of young boys succeeding to the title. Four
generations of counts, starting with Johann Willem Friso's grandfather
and ending with his son, died leaving an underage boy as the heir.
Willem IV died at forty, and was succeeded by a three-year-old. This
pattern empowered the women in the family, as the boys' mothers
usually acted as regent until they came of age. Johann Willem Friso's
widow, Marie Luise of Hesse-Kassel, was the regent twice – first for
her son and later for her grandson. In Holland she was called *Marijke
Meu*, or Aunt Mary[13]. There are not many examples in the Holy Roman

Empire of a female ruler in her own right, but it was not uncommon for a widowed mother to rule as regent on behalf of her son.

After Albertine Agnes died in 1696 the next owner of Oranienstein was her widowed daughter-in-law, who was also her niece, Henriette Amalie. She converted Oranienstein into the baroque palace we see today and installed the beautiful plasterwork and painted ceilings which are such a feature of the schloss. Our tour started in the stunning *Cour D'Honneur* (courtyard in front of the schloss) which has the initials of Henriette Amalie and a golden crown over the entrance gate. Henriette Amalie moved into Oranienstein with her six unmarried daughters, and our guide joked that they liked to sit on the balcony at the end of this courtyard and direct the servants on the cobbled squares as if they were chess pieces (see illustration 77).

After the last unmarried daughter died in 1771, Oranienstein wasn't used much by the Nassau-Diez (now Nassau-Orange) family who spent most of their time in the Netherlands. After the Napoleonic Wars the schloss became part of the duchy of Nassau, ruled by another branch of the family, and when Nassau was annexed in 1866 it became Prussian. There is a small section in the museum commemorating the years (1867-1920) that Oranienstein served as a Prussian Cadet School (see Bensberg in chapter two). The princes of Orange were

79. The chapel at Oranienstein is serene and filled with light.

stadholders of the Dutch republic until they were ousted when French Revolutionary troops invaded in 1795, and the Netherlands became a satellite of France. At the end of the Napoleonic Wars the Netherlands became a monarchy, with Willem VI of Orange as King Willem I.

Grafenschloss Diez

Grafenschloss Diez was the residence of the counts of Nassau-Diez before Albertine Agnes built Oranienstein. It towers above the town of Diez and is extremely photogenic. The oldest part dates back to the eleventh century, and the newer parts to the eighteenth century when it was used as a prison and workhouse. Today the schloss houses a Youth Hostel and restaurant, as well as a museum. In the courtyard is a fountain erected in 1716 by Henriette Amalie in memory of her son, Johann Willem Friso, who drowned in Holland.

The museum was closed for lunch, but the curator happened to notice us in the courtyard and came out for a chat. He also very kindly allowed us to take a quick look inside and gave me a charming memento when we left. This was a small coin – a three and a half 'Diezer' piece (not real currency) that the museum mints for children.

I didn't know much about the history of the Dutch royal family before my visit to Oranienstein and it was a surprise to learn that, like so many of Europe's other royal families; they also originated in a little German principality. The museum has a huge family tree, and many portraits – from Prince Willem I of Orange (1533-1584) to King Willem-Alexander (born in 1967). Some of the portraits, including those of Albertine Agnes and Henriette Amalie, hang in the elegant Blue and Gold Salon, which has blue paintwork and golden pilasters using colours from the crest of the Dutch royal family. This large room was the ballroom and has a semi-circular window at one end (the former apse of the old monastery church) and one of the beautiful plasterwork ceilings that are a legacy of Henriette Amalie. The last room on the tour was the serene and light-filled chapel. This has lavish decoration including a magnificent ceiling fresco of the miracle of Pentecost, when the Holy Spirit descended on the Apostles.

Our guided tour of Oranienstein was a great success. The schloss is in tip-top condition and very well maintained by the German Army. The only drawback was that the English handout for the tour was woefully short, and the guide spoke no English. But this was understandable, as most visitors are Dutch and the guides have to be bi-lingual in Dutch and German. At the end of the tour there was another nice surprise in the small garden overlooking the river Lahn. Our guide pointed out a two-hundred-year-old tulip tree and said it was in bloom. The flowers of this tree (Latin name liriodendron tulipifera) are inconspicuous, so I went closer to take a look. And there they were – lots of them – delicate and pale green.

Stolzenfels

Stolzenfels is a dramatic landmark that dominates the Rhine south of Koblenz. The photo in illustration 80 was taken from several miles away, on the other side of the river. Painted yellow and framed by trees, the schloss seems to hang on the cliff-side of the left bank of the Rhine Gorge, high above the river. I first saw Stolzenfels from the terrace at Schloss Marksburg (on the opposite bank), when I was researching my first book. Since then I had always wanted to visit this schloss.

Stolzenfels was a ruin when it was given to Crown Prince Friedrich Wilhelm of Prussia by the city of Koblenz in 1823. They had previously tried to sell it but without any luck, even though the price was cheap[14]. It was an astute gift: the Rhineland had only become a Prussian province in 1815 (it was awarded to Prussia at the Congress of Vienna) and the nineteen-year-old crown prince had been completely bowled over by his first trip along the river in that same year. 'On past all those thousand divine castles and cliffs and mountains and currents;' he wrote 'I was weary with bliss.'[15] Friedrich Wilhelm was a romantic and had a passionate love of history. He would rebuild Stolzenfels to embody his ideas of medieval chivalry and courtly life.

80. Stolzenfels is a dramatic landmark that dominates the Rhine south of Koblenz.

The original Stolzenfels was built between 1242 and 1259 by Arnold von Isenburg, the archbishop-elector of Trier. The electorate of Trier had territory on both banks of the Rhine around Koblenz. Stolzenfels is a *Hangburg* (a castle on a hillside) and was built on an outcrop of land on the steep cliff of the gorge, above the village of Kapellen. Its original purpose was as a customs post, to collect river tolls from the passing river traffic. At this time there were dozens of customs posts along the Rhine and castle owners extended ropes or chains across the river to enforce collection of their toll[16]. After the right to collect river taxes moved elsewhere, Stolzenfels was used as a residence by the archbishop-electors of Trier. Because of its location (at a point where the lands of the three ecclesiastical electorates touched), it was sometimes used as the venue for pre-meetings of electors prior to the election of the Holy Roman emperor. The formal election, with all the electors, took place at the Königsstuhl (Royal Throne) in nearby Rhens. The election of Emperor Karl IV in 1346 was the outcome of preliminary discussions held at Stolzenfels by the archbishop-electors of Cologne, Mainz, and Trier and the prince-elector of the Palatine[17].

Like other medieval castles along the Rhine, Stolzenfels was defended by high walls and a moat. Long walls also connected it to the fortified village of Kapellen on the riverside. The original Stolzenfels was burned down in 1689, by French troops besieging Koblenz at the start of the War of the Palatine Succession. King Louis XIV of France had long cast covetous eyes on the Rhineland and his pretext for starting this war was to pursue the inheritance claims of his sister-in-law, born a princess of the Palatine (the electorate of the Palatine had territory in the Rhineland). The burnt-out shell was further destroyed when the schloss was then used as a quarry and source of building materials. The demolition by local builders in 1801 of a long wall connecting it to the river is an example of this[18].

In 1803 the ruins were transferred to the ownership of the city of Koblenz, as part of the abolition of the church states, including the electorate of Trier, and the secularisation of their lands. Twenty years later the city fathers gave it to the crown prince after they heard of his interest in acquiring a Rhine castle. Their new province seemed to exert a fascination over the Prussian royal family and Stolzenfels would become one of a whole clutch of ruined Rhine castles they would acquire. The first mover was the crown prince's cousin, known in the family as Fritz Luis, who purchased Schloss Rheinstein in 1823. It was a list of available ruins drawn up for Fritz Louis that triggered the idea of the gift of Stolzenfels with the city fathers[19]. The crown prince also bought Stahleck in 1828 and Sooneck, jointly with his three brothers, in 1834.

The Königsstuhl

The Königsstuhl (or Royal Throne) is an extraordinary-looking structure at Rhens, on the left bank of the Rhine, two miles south of Stolzenfels. This was the place where, by tradition, the seven electors of the Holy Roman Empire

met to cast their votes and enthrone the new Holy Roman emperor. The original wooden structure dated back to the fourteenth century, but in the seventeenth century it was rebuilt in stone, as an eight-sided platform open to the skies. Each of the seven electors could be seated against one wall, and the eighth side contained the entry to the platform.

Courtesy of Franz-Josef Schmillen.

When the army of the French Revolution occupied the left bank of the Rhine, the Royal Throne had long fallen out of use and was in bad repair. The French demolished it in 1804, to make way for a road, and sold off the stones. It was rebuilt in 1842, funded by public subscription with a top-up from King Friedrich Wilhelm IV of Prussia[20]. It is not clear how far this structure resembles its predecessors, as the historical evidence is thin.

The throne was always located out in the open, so that the electors could not be influenced or leant on[21]. But in 1929 it was moved from the bank of the Rhine to a new location on the top of the river cliff. There it feels rather detached and no-one else came to visit it while we were there.

Friedrich Wilhelm had plans drawn up to restore Stolzenfels, but also considered leaving it as a romantic ruin. It was not until 1835 that he finally decided to rebuild the schloss as a holiday home for himself and his wife (he had married Princess Elisabeth of Bavaria in 1823). The prince instructed that the ruins of the old schloss

'...should be protected as far as possible, and a complete whole should be restored on the foundations in accordance with the needs of the present day.'[22] But in reality the new Stolzenfels is a different schloss to the old. Around the end of the nineteenth century a heated debate would begin about the best way to preserve ruins and the difference between 'preservation', 'restoration', and 'rebuilding'.

Stolzenfels was always too small to house the paraphernalia of a court and the king's household had to stay elsewhere (the crown prince became King Friedrich Wilhelm IV of Prussia in 1840). Instead, Friedrich Wilhelm created a make-believe medieval world where he could escape into his version of the past. When he and his wife arrived at Kapellen by boat for the formal opening of the schloss in 1842, they were greeted by local craftsmen in old German dress who made a presentation and sang songs. A torchlight

81. King Friedrich Wilhelm IV of Prussia and his wife, Elisabeth of Bavaria.

procession, several hundred strong, accompanied the royal couple up the winding path to the schloss.

As visitors we took the same steep path, which winds and twists up the side of the gorge. There is only one way into the schloss – across a dry moat, through the Inner Castle Gateway, and into the Inner Courtyard. For me the glory of Stolzenfels was the gardens, and from this narrow courtyard, enclosed by the high walls of the schloss, there is a first glimpse of the Pergola Garden through an open arcade of three tall gothic arches, called the Arcade Hall. The arches are supported by slender pillars and these produce an interesting visual effect, because they get longer as they march down the steps towards the garden.

The Pergola Garden is small, but wow (!) has the designer made the best use of the space. A crenelated wall encloses this semi-circular garden and under it runs the pergola, from which it gets its name. In the middle is a fountain surrounded by a pattern of gravel paths and small beds in the shape of a rose window from a gothic cathedral. The beds were planted with spring tulips and edged with low hedging when we were there. The Pergola Garden has the feeling of a stage set, and I almost expected a character from Shakespeare to make an entrance through one of the arches in the wall. In 1845, the German artist Caspar Scheuren painted a series of twelve watercolours of the schloss in which it is inhabited by an imaginary medieval court. His picture of the Pergola Garden includes courtiers in medieval dress lounging about; in that of the Arcade Hall, a medieval watchman asleep on the steps.

82. A romantic painting of Stolzenfels as a ruin (before it was rebuilt by Friedrich Wilhelm IV) with exaggeratedly high walls and set off by a rainbow.

The room I liked the best at Stolzenfels is also in the garden. The Summer Hall occupies the cellar of the wing facing the Rhine and has wide doors that open directly onto a large patio called the Rhine Terrace. At the front of this terrace the cliff drops steeply away and the views of the river, both downstream (towards the sea) in the direction of Koblenz and upstream to Marksburg, are just amazing. The Summer Hall was used as a dining room in summer and has blue and white tiled walls and a vaulted ceiling, to keep it cool. Another of the watercolours by Scheuren shows the make-believe medieval court at table in the Summer Hall, where they are being served by pages. The sun streams through the open doors, but the hall is cool and shady.

Stolzenfels is the last schloss in this book and is not too far from the first – which was Augustusburg at Brühl. The distance by road is about sixty-five miles, but a shorter route is by river and that's how Queen Victoria travelled between the two. When Victoria left Augustusburg after her visit in August 1842 (see chapter two), the next stop on her German tour was Stolzenfels. The royal party (including Victoria and her husband Albert, and Friedrich Wilhelm IV and his wife Elisabeth), took the train to Bonn and boarded a Rhine steamboat for the rest of the journey. Victoria wrote in her journal how they could see everything from their seats at the front of the boat and how at every turn of the river there was another beautiful view.

She described Stolzenfels as '...this Bijou [jewel] of a castle situated in the most beautiful Position imaginable...' and said she was so enchanted with the Rhine that, looking out of the windows of the schloss, she could sing 'Mein Herz ist am Rhein'[23]. (*My Heart is on the Rhine* was a popular German song published in 1841. The last line of each verse goes 'Wherever I am, wherever I go, my heart is on the Rhine.')

Victoria and Albert stayed in the Prussian royal couple's private apartments on the first floor of the schloss. These were arranged as a suite of rooms for Queen Elisabeth in the wing facing the Rhine and another for Friedrich Wilhelm IV in the wing behind it facing the hill. The rooms are decorated in fashionable mid-nineteenth-century neo-gothic and Victoria thought them '...quite lovely and beautifully furnished'[24]. To me they seemed small and dark with wood panelling, dark wallpaper, and heavy furniture. In the king's wing there was clear damage from subsidence of the building, with large cracks in the walls and sloping floors. The curator explained that the problem has now been fixed, but the rooms still require renovation.

The king's and queen's suites are connected by a room over the Arcade Hall, that Friedrich Wilhelm and Elisabeth shared as a bedroom. Here the curator pointed out the rondels in the stained glass window, with the coats-of-arms of Queen Victoria and Prince Albert. These were a gift from the British royal couple to their hosts, commemorating the visit. The Common Bedroom is the most romantic looking room in the schloss. In her journal, Victoria said Friedrich Wilhelm and Elisabeth were touchingly fond of each other and she had seen them kiss, like a young married couple[25].

83. Stolzenfels seen from Kapellen, at the bottom of the cliff, with the chapel in front.

On the first night of Victoria's stay there was a massive firework display over the Rhine, watched by spectators on both banks, and also crowded onto steamers on the river. One set-piece showed the burning initials of the two queens (Victoria and Elisabeth) with an English lion to one side, a Prussian eagle to the other, and all surmounted by a royal crown. In another, 2500 rockets were released into the sky from a meadow on the opposite bank of the river[26]. On the second evening the royal party were entertained by a star-studded concert in the Great Knights' Hall, where the musicians included the celebrated composer Giacomo Meyerbeer, the virtuoso pianist Franz Liszt, and the famous singer Jenny Lind[27].

The Great Knights' Hall is the larger of the two entertaining rooms on the ground floor of the schloss (the other is the Small Knights' Hall). The high vaulted ceiling is supported by two tall pillars in the centre of the room and the dining table had to be specially constructed around them. The walls are decorated with displays of old weaponry and armour which, according to my late-nineteenth-century guidebook to the Rhine, included the swords of Napoleon I and of Field Marshals Murat and Blücher[28]. Between the two halls is the main staircase, the smallest I have seen in any schloss. This is a spiral staircase with a most unusual feature – it has no central newel post!

Stolzenfels is an expression of the personality of its builder, Friedrich Wilhelm IV. But the king had many other schlösser, and he only visited his beloved holiday home seven times[29]. In later life he suffered from ill-health and became disabled following a series of strokes. In 1858 he was deemed unfit to rule and his younger brother, Wilhelm, was appointed regent. Wilhelm was also his brother's heir, as Friedrich Wilhelm and Elisabeth had no children. King Friedrich Wilhelm IV of Prussia died in 1861.

8

REFLECTIONS

In the last three years I have been fortunate to visit over one hundred schlösser in the course of researching my books. At the beginning it was a longstanding interest in European royal history that took me to see them, but soon I was also fascinated by the history of the wonderful buildings themselves. Schlösser were the setting where history was made, and a lasting legacy of the desire of princes to display their wealth and power.

The schlösser in my books were built over a long range of time – from the romanesque Kaiserpfalz Goslar in Lower Saxony in *Schloss II* (built in the first years of the eleventh century to house the travelling court of the early Holy Roman emperors), to historicist Cecilienhof in Potsdam in *Schloss* (built in imitation of an English country house in the twilight years of the monarchy in the early twentieth century, as the summer residence of the kaiser's eldest son).

Over the centuries these buildings have survived war, fire, and neglect and were continually remodelled to meet the changing needs and fashions of the day. Stolzenfels (in chapter seven of this book) was a ruin until it was rebuilt by Friedrich Wilhelm IV, and Kaiserpfalz Goslar had been used as a storage barn before it was rescued by his brother, Kaiser Wilhelm I. The schloss in Braunschweig (*Schloss II*) burned down and was rebuilt three times, most recently in 2007 when it opened as a shopping centre! Altenstein (see chapter five in this book) was built as a baroque palace in the 1730s; remodelled one hundred and fifty years later as a neo-renaissance country house; and is currently under renovation as a Brahms museum following a devastating fire in 1982.

But perhaps it is the hundred years since World War I that have brought the greatest challenges to the survival of schlösser. Four years of gruelling conflict destroyed the fabric of pre-war society and revolution toppled the German monarchy in November 1918. Without their ruling princes these large buildings lost the main purposes for which they were designed and suddenly their future looked uncertain. During the Weimar Republic there was a political movement to expropriate the property of the ex-ruling houses, but in the end it was left for each new Free State to reach agreement with the old royal family.

By and large these agreements treated the families generously. At Bückeburg (see *Schloss II*) the princes of Schaumburg-Lippe were permitted to keep their ancestral schloss but obliged to open it to the public as a museum. Even the ex-kaiser's family retained residence rights at Cecilienhof, although actual ownership was taken over by the state. But in a few cases the matter was not easily settled and in the State of Lippe a dispute rumbled on for years. Prince Leopold IV of Lippe tried to sit out the revolution in his schloss at Detmold (see chapter two) until he was dispossessed and thrown out by revolutionaries and the schloss taken over by the state. It was not until 1937 that an agreement between the Lippe family and the State of Lippe was reached under which Detmold was returned to Leopold IV[1].

Many schlösser were damaged or destroyed by bombing in World War II. All of the Hesse-Darmstadt schlösser in the centre of Darmstadt, including the Grand Ducal Schloss (chapter six), were destroyed in a single night on 11 September 1944. Over the seventy years since World War II, many schlösser have been restored or rebuilt, but others may be lost forever due to lack of money. In the immediate post-war years there were other burning priorities, and no mood in Dessau to restore the schloss when resources were so desperately needed for housing and infrastructure (see Johannbau in chapter four). In the 1960s the schloss in Kiel (*Schloss II*) was one of the first to be reconstructed. But, in a deliberate break with the past, it was rebuilt as a modern block and not to how it looked before the war.

The enormous costs involved in maintaining and reconstructing these buildings are a huge barrier. Over the decades, several proposals for Schloss Schwarzburg (*Schloss II*), gutted and left uninhabitable by Hitler, foundered for lack of funding. The schloss is now being restored and due to be completed in 2019. But the solutions may not always seem attractive: the decision to rebuild Braunschweig was hugely controversial because of the plan to make the schloss commercially viable by using it as a shopping centre. One of the latest to be rebuilt, in 2013, is an ancestral schloss of the British royal family, at Herrenhausen in Hannover (see *Schloss*). This was funded by the Volkswagen Foundation.

A further challenge in the difficult twentieth century fell to those schlösser behind the Iron Curtain when Germany was divided after World War II. These were expropriated and put to use as all sorts of institutions including barracks, refugee camps, schools, and hospitals. Mirow in the Mecklenburg Lake District was used an old people's home, and Rheinsberg in neighbouring Brandenburg, as a sanatorium (both *Schloss II*). Very often these years are glossed over in the information for today's visitors. Wiligrad in Mecklenburg was a military-style police academy, and Rochlitz in Saxony an interrogation centre for the Soviet secret police (both *Schloss*). With their contents dissipated and interiors altered to fit their new use, these schlösser behind the Iron Curtain suffered neglect and deterioration for nearly half a century.

But fifty years is a relatively short time in the history of schlösser and, since the fall of the Iron Curtain, many have already been rescued and restored. The fortunes of Mirow turned for the better when it was acquired by the new state government, and after years of restoration it opened as a museum in 2014. After reunification there was a hope that expropriated schlösser might be returned to their old owners, but restitution was not straightforward. The von Stralendorff family had owned Schloss Gamehl in Mecklenburg (*Schloss I*) for more than five hundred and fifty years until it was expropriated at the end of World War II. After failed negotiations with the local authority, they eventually bought it back for market value at auction in 2001. During the Soviet years the schloss housed several families, a kindergarten, shop, and post office. Today, after a careful restoration which took seven years, it is a stylish and comfortable small hotel.

Even pre-war owners who might have had a claim did not always pursue this. When the Saxe-Coburg-Gotha family reached agreement with the State of Thuringia regarding compensation for their pre-war assets, they preferred to accept forestry land rather than restitution of their Thuringian schlösser[2]. Schloss Reinhardsbrunn at Friedrichroda (*Schloss II*) belonged to the family until it was confiscated in 1945. Today it lies empty, stripped-out, and abandoned; in desperate need of an owner willing to make the large investment to restore it.

The challenge for schlösser in the twenty-first century is to find a commercial use and be self-supporting. Many have reinvented themselves and are thriving; others such as Reinhardsbrunn are still struggling to secure their survival. During my visits as part of researching the books, I have been able to make my own observations on how schlösser are being used today. The results are shown for each schloss in the list in appendix B, and summarised overall in illustration 84. The majority of the schlösser on my list (58%) are now used solely or primarily as museums, but a surprising 31.5% make their living in a different way. (Of the balance, 4.5% are empty or destroyed, 3% under renovation, and 3% in private occupation – for example Rastede Schloss in *Schloss II*).

The most common of the other uses are two that are closest to how schlösser were originally used in the princes' day – as government

84. How schlösser are used today.

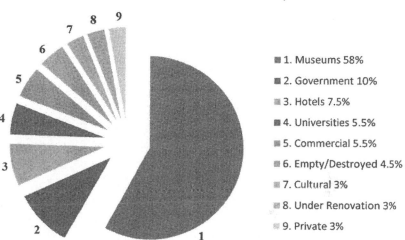

1. Museums 58%

2. Government 10%

3. Hotels 7.5%

4. Universities 5.5%

5. Commercial 5.5%

6. Empty/Destroyed 4.5%

7. Cultural 3%

8. Under Renovation 3%

9. Private 3%

Each schloss has been allocated according to the author's observation of its sole or main use. The percentages have been rounded.

buildings (10%) and hotels including youth hostels (7.5%). Schlösser that look to be in best repair are often those in public ownership (because they have access to government money). These include Oranienstein (chapter seven) which is home to the Army Medical Care Command, and Schwerin (in *Schloss*) which houses the Mecklenburg-Western Pomerania state parliament. As the venue for state visits to the Federal Republic of Germany (West Germany), Augustusburg near Bonn (chapter two) was kept in sparkling condition.

Writing about schlösser is an excellent reason for staying in schloss hotels and some of our favourites include the Taschenbergpalais in Dresden (*Schloss*), Schloss Blücher in the Mecklenburg Lake District (*Schloss II*), Häcker's Grand Hotel in the Bathhouse Palace, Bad Ems (this book), and of course Friedrichshof in the Taunus Hills near Frankfurt (*Schloss*).

But as you can see from the pie chart in illustration 84, there are many other uses for schlösser too. My husband and I have also visited an artist's colony, an auction house, a small business centre, events venues, cultural centres, universities, parks and gardens, a law court, a library of books on castles, a shopping centre, and of course (see Oranienstein) an Army base.

From among the twenty-five schlösser in this book I do, of course, have favourites. For me Mosigkau was a special place where everything about my visit was just right – fascinating family history, wonderful contents, and a really nice guide. Other favourites are the Wartburg, because a visit there is like walking through the pages of a history book; Wilhelmsthal, as a masterpiece of rococo art; and Oranienstein, because it was such a surprise and I learnt about the history of the Dutch royal family. But my overall favourite has to be Augustusburg, the magnificent baroque summer palace at Brühl built by one of the great princes of his age to show off his wealth and power.

The author's favourite schlösser in this book

Augustusburg in North Rhine-Westphalia
Mosigkau in Saxony-Anhalt
The Wartburg in Thuringia
Wilhelmsthal in Hesse
Oranienstein in Rhineland-Palatinate

When Queen Victoria left Stolzenfels after her visit in August 1842, she continued to cruise up the Rhine to her next destination, which was the Hotel de L'Europe in Mainz. Victoria travelled on her own steam-boat called *The Fairy*, which was the tender to the royal yacht and had come out from England with her. *The Fairy* apparently caused a sensation on the Rhine because it had superior technology to the German vessels[3]. My husband and I left Stolzenfels by car, to start the long drive back to our home in Cornwall, in the south-west of England. But we will be back again to explore schlösser in Bavaria, in southern Germany, for my next book.

APPENDICES

Appendix A: Map of Germany

The map opposite (which is hand drawn) shows the sixteen federal states of Germany and the approximate location of the twenty-five schlösser included in this book. Please use the list below to match the numbers with the individual schlösser.

1. Augustusburg
2. Nordkirchen
3. Bensberg
4. Burg Vischering
5. Burg Altena
6. Detmold
7. Pyrmont
8. Bevern
9. Johannbau
10. Mosigkau
11. Wörlitz Country House
12. Quedlinburg Abbey Castle
13. The Wartburg
14. Elisabethenburg
15. Altenstein
16. Wilhelmsburg
17. Grand Ducal Schloss, Darmstadt
18. Jagdschloss Kranichstein
19. Heiligenberg
20. Burg Friedberg
21. Wilhelmshöhe
22. Wilhelmsthal
23. Bathhouse Palace, Bad Ems
24. Oranienstein
25. Stolzenfels

Appendix B: List of the schlösser included in my books

Name (location if different)	Family	Current use	Book
Berlin & Brandenburg			
Altes Palais (Berlin)	Hohenzollern	University	I
Cecilienhof (Potsdam)	Hohenzollern	Museum & Hotel (closed)	I
Charlottenburg (Berlin)	Hohenzollern	Museum	I
Kronprinzenpalais (Berlin)	Hohenzollern	Under renovation	I
Neues Palais (Potsdam)	Hohenzollern	Museum	I
New Pavilion (Berlin)	Hohenzollern	Museum	I
Paretz (Ketzin)	Hohenzollern	Museum	I
Rheinsberg	Hohenzollern	Museum	II
Sanssouci (Potsdam)	Hohenzollern	Museum	I
Hesse			
Bad Homburg	Hesse-Homburg	Museum	I
Burgruine Königstein	Nassau	Museum	I
Darmstadt	Hesse-Darmstadt	University/empty, Museum	III
Friedberg	Hesse-Darmstadt	Government offices	III
Friedrichshof (Kronberg i/Taunus)	Hesse-Kassel	Hotel	I
Heiligenberg (Jugenheim)	Battenberg	Business centre, Museum	III
Kranichstein (Darmstadt)	Hesse-Darmstadt	Museum & Hotel	III
Kronberg	Lords of Kronberg	Museum	I
Luxembourg (Königstein i/Taunus)	Nassau	Law Court	I
Rosenhöhe (Darmstadt)	Hesse-Darmstadt	Gardens	III
Wilhelmshöhe (Kassel)	Hesse-Kassel	Museum	III
Wilhelmsthal (Calden)	Hesse-Kassel	Museum & Events venue	III
Wolfsgarten (Langen)	Hesse-Darmstadt	Private	III
Lower Saxony			
Ahlden	Hannover	Auction house	I
Bevern	Brunswick-Bevern	Museum	III
Braunschweig	Brunswick-Wolfenbüttel	Shopping centre, Museum	II
Bückeburg	Schaumburg-Lippe	Museum	II
Celle	Hannover	Museum	I
Fallersleben (Wolfsburg)	Brunswick-Lüneburg	Museum	II
Herrenhausen (Hannover)	Hannover	Gardens	I
Jever	Anhalt-Zerbst	Museum	II
Kaiserpfalz (Goslar)	Holy Roman Emperors	Museum	II
Marienburg (Pattensen)	Hannover	Museum	I
Oldenburg	Oldenburg	Museum	II

Pyrmont	Waldeck-Pyrmont	Museum	III
Rastede Palais	Oldenburg	Museum	II
Rastede Schloss	Oldenburg	Private	II
Little Richmond (Braunschweig)	Brunswick-Wolfenbüttel	Events venue & Park	II
Salzdahlum	Brunswick-Wolfenbüttel	Destroyed	II
Stadthagen	Holstein-Schaumburg	Government offices, Museum	II
Wolfenbüttel	Brunswick-Wolfenbüttel	Museum & School	II
Wolfsburg	Schulenburg-Wolfsburg	Cultural centre, Museum	II

Mecklenburg-Pomerania

Bad Doberan	Mecklenburg-Schwerin	Government offices	I
Blücher (Göhren-Lebbin)	Blücher	Hotel	II
Gamehl	von Stralendorff	Hotel	I
Gelbensande	Mecklenburg-Schwerin	Restaurant & Museum	I
Güstrow	Mecklenburg-Güstrow	Museum	I
Hohenzieritz	Mecklenburg-Strelitz	Offices & Museum	II
Ludwigslust	Mecklenburg-Schwerin	Museum	I
Mirow	Mecklenburg-Strelitz	Museum	II
Neustrelitz	Mecklenburg-Strelitz	Destroyed	II
Prinzenpalais (Bad Doberan)	Mecklenburg-Schwerin	Hotel	I
Schwerin	Mecklenburg-Schwerin	State Parliament, Museum	I
Burg Stargard	Mecklenburg-Strelitz	Museum, Hotel, Restaurant	II
Wiligrad (Löbstorf)	Mecklenburg-Schwerin	Artists' colony	I

North Rhine-Westphalia

Altena	von Mark	Museum	III
Augustusburg (Brühl)	Wittelsbach	Museum	III
Bensberg (Bergisch-Gladbach)	Wittelsbach	Hotel	III
Clemensruhe (Bonn)	Wittelsbach	University	III
Detmold	Lippe	Museum	III
Electoral Palace (Bonn)	Wittelsbach	University	III
Falkenlust (Brühl)	Wittelsbach	Museum	III
Nordkirchen	von Plettenberg	University	III
Türnich (Kerpen)	von Hoensbroech	Market Garden, Café	III
Vischering (Lüdinghausen)	zu Vischering	Museum	III

Rhineland-Palatinate

Bathhouse Palace (Bad Ems)	Nassau-Diez	Hotel	III
Diez	Nassau-Diez	Youth hostel, Museum	III
Marksburg (Braubach)	Hesse/Nassau	Museum, Castles Assn	I
Oranienstein (Diez)	Nassau-Diez	Army base, Museum	III
Philippsburg (Braubach)	Hesse-Rheinfels	Library, Research Institute	I
Stolzenfels (Koblenz)	Hohenzollern	Museum	III
Vier Turme (Bad Ems)	von Thüngen	Government offices	III

Saxony

Burg Stolpen	Wettin	Museum	I
Colditz	Wettin	Museum, Youth hostel	I
Pillnitz (Dresden)	Wettin	Museum	I
Residenzschloss (Dresden)	Wettin	Museum	I
Rochlitz	Wettin	Museum	I
Taschenbergpalais (Dresden)	Wettin	Hotel	I

Saxony Anhalt

Bernburg	Anhalt-Bernburg	Museum	III
Luisium (Dessau)	Anhalt-Dessau	Museum, Park	III
Johannbau (Dessau)	Anhalt-Dessau	Museum, Café	III
Mosigkau	Anhalt-Dessau	Museum	III
Oranienbaum	Anhalt-Dessau	Museum, Park	III
Quedlinburg	Abbesses of Quedlinburg	Museum	III
Wörlitz	Anhalt-Dessau	Museum, Park	III

Schleswig-Holstein

Blomenburg (Selent)	von Blome	Empty	II
Eutin	Holstein-Gottorf	Museum	II
Glücksburg	Holstein-Glücksburg	Museum	II
Gottorf	Holstein-Gottorf	Museum	II
Hemmelmark	Hohenzollern	Private	II
Husum	Holstein-Gottorf	Museum	II
Kiel	Hohenzollern	Concert hall	II
Salzau (Fargau-Pratjau)	von Blome	Empty	II

Thuringia

Altenstein (Bad Liebenstein)	Saxe-Meiningen	Under renovation, gardens	III
Belvedere (Weimar)	Saxe-Weimar-Eisenach	Museum	II
Elisabethenburg (Meiningen)	Saxe-Meiningen	Museum	III
Friedenstein (Gotha)	Saxe-Gotha-Altenburg	Museum, Gov't, Theatre	II
Heidecksburg (Rudolstadt)	Schwarzburg-Rudolstadt	Museum	II
Palais Weimar (Bad Liebenstein)	Saxe-Meiningen	Library	III
Reinhardsbrunn (Friedrichroda)	Saxe-Coburg-Gotha	Empty	II
Residenzschloss (Weimar)	Saxe-Weimar-Eisenach	Museum	II
Saalfeld	Saxe-Coburg-Saalfeld	Government offices	II
Schwarzburg	Schwarzburg-Rudolstadt	Under renovation, Museum	II
Wartburg (Eisenach)	Ludovingian	Museum, Hotel	III
Wilhelmsburg (Schmalkalden)	Hesse-Kassel	Museum	III

1. The list of schlösser is organised in alphabetical order by federal state and, within each state, in alphabetical order by schloss.

2. Where the schloss does not have the same name as the town or village in which it is located, the location is shown in brackets in the left hand column entitled 'Name'. For example in Hesse, Kranichstein is located in Darmstadt.

3. The column entitled 'Family' shows the name of the royal or noble family with which the author most associates the schloss. Schlösser which were Imperial Palaces are listed as 'Holy Roman Emperors'; and Quedlinburg, which was an abbey ruled by an abbess, is shown as 'Abbesses of Quedlinburg'.

4. In the interests of space, a small number of family names have been abbreviated; for example Schleswig-Holstein-Glücksburg has been shortened to Holstein-Glücksburg.

5. Entries in the column entitled 'Current use' are based on the author's observations when visiting each schloss as part of researching the books. Major (but not necessarily all) uses are recorded.

6. The right hand side column ('Which book') indicates in which of the author's three books on schlösser (Schloss(I), Schloss II(II), and Schloss III(III)) a particular schloss is included.

Appendix C: List of Germany's royal families

In 1815, at the end of the Napoleonic Wars, the political map of Europe was redrawn at the Congress of Vienna. The congress created a new alliance of German and Central European states called the German Confederation, under the presidency of Austria. The list below shows the thirty-one sovereign states in Germany that were members of the Confederation, indicating which of these appear in which of my books.

It should be noted that my books also include further royal states that were no longer in existence by 1815, either because they had previously been abolished (for example the electorate of Cologne), or the royal family had become extinct (for example the county of Mark).

Anhalt-Dessau	III	Oldenburg	II
Anhalt-Bernburg	III	Prussia	I,II,III
Anhalt-Köthen		Reuss, elder line	
Baden		Reuss, younger line	
Bavaria	III	Saxe-Coburg-Saalfeld	II
Brunswick	II	Saxe-Gotha-Altenburg	II
Hannover	I	Saxe-Hildburghausen	
Hesse-Darmstadt	III	Saxe-Meiningen	III
Hesse-Homburg	I	Saxe-Weimar-Eisenach	II
Hesse-Kassel	III	Saxony	I
Hohenzollern-Hechingen		Schaumburg-Lippe	II
Hohenzollern-Sigmaringen		Schwarzburg-Rudolstadt	II
Lippe	III	Schwarzburg-Sonderhausen	
Mecklenburg-Schwerin	I	Waldeck-Pyrmont	III
Mecklenburg-Strelitz	II	Württemberg	
Nassau	I		

List taken from Wikipedia, the free encyclopaedia. German Confederation. Note (4), Heeren, Arnold Hermann Ludwig (1873), Talboys, David Alphonso, ed.; *A Manual of the History of the Political System of Europe and its Colonies* (London: H.G. Bohn), 480–481.

Appendix D: Charts and family trees

1. The Bavarian branch of the Wittelsbach family showing the electors of Bavaria and the archbishop-electors of Cologne.
2. The disputed succession to the principality of Lippe.
3. The daughters of Prince Georg Viktor of Waldeck-Pyrmont.
4. The marriages and children of King Willem III of the Netherlands.
5. The succession to the duchy of Brunswick-Wolfenbüttel, from August der Jüngere to Karl I.
6. A simplified history of the Anhalt principalities.
7. Family tree for the princes of Anhalt-Dessau from 'Der Alte Dessauer' to 'Vater Franz'.
8. The Ludovingian dynasty and the landgraves of Thuringia.
9. The eleven dukes of Saxe-Meiningen.
10. The relationship between the Hesse-Darmstadt and Battenberg families.
11. The children of Princess Alice of Great Britain.
12. Family tree for the Battenbergs.
13. The landgraves of Hesse-Kassel and the builders of Wilhelmshöhe and Wilhelmsthal.
14. The four princesses of Orange and their schlösser.
15. How the counts of Nassau-Diez became the Dutch royal line.

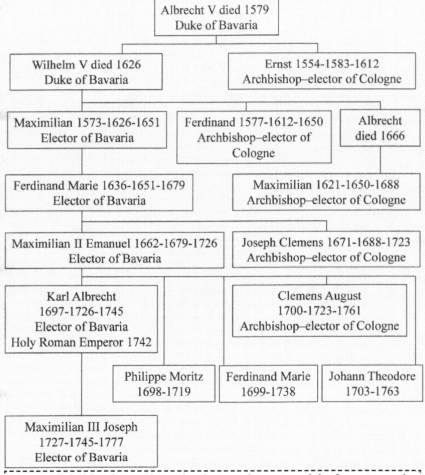

**1. THE BAVARIAN BRANCH OF THE WITTELSBACH FAMILY
SHOWING THE ELECTORS OF BAVARIA AND
THE ARCHBISHOP-ELECTORS OF COLOGNE**

Albrecht V died 1579
Duke of Bavaria

Wilhelm V died 1626
Duke of Bavaria

Ernst 1554-1583-1612
Archbishop–elector of Cologne

Maximilian 1573-1626-1651
Elector of Bavaria

Ferdinand 1577-1612-1650
Archbishop–elector of
Cologne

Albrecht
died 1666

Ferdinand Marie 1636-1651-1679
Elector of Bavaria

Maximilian 1621-1650-1688
Archbishop–elector of Cologne

Maximilian II Emanuel 1662-1679-1726
Elector of Bavaria

Joseph Clemens 1671-1688-1723
Archbishop–elector of Cologne

Karl Albrecht
1697-1726-1745
Elector of Bavaria
Holy Roman Emperor 1742

Clemens August
1700-1723-1761
Archbishop–elector of Cologne

Philippe Moritz
1698-1719

Ferdinand Marie
1699-1738

Johann Theodore
1703-1763

Maximilian III Joseph
1727-1745-1777
Elector of Bavaria

> This simplified family tree shows the electors of Bavaria and the five princes who were archbishop-electors of Cologne in succession. It does not show all family members, but does show the five sons of Elector Maximilian II Emanuel. Where three dates are given, these are dates of (1) birth, (2) start of reign, and (3) death.

2. THE DISPUTED SUCCESSION TO THE PRINCIPALITY OF LIPPE

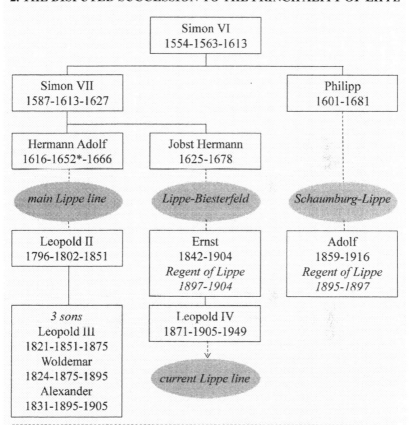

This simplified chart indicates the origins of three branches of the House of Lippe. Dotted lines mean that generations have been omitted. The two elder sons of Leopold II were both married but neither couple had children and the main Lippe line died out with Prince Alexander. He was declared unfit to rule and when he succeeded in 1895 there was a legal battle for the regency. * Hermann Adolf was the third son of Simon VII to rule and succeeded his elder brother in 1652

3. THE DAUGHTERS OF PRINCE GEORG VIKTOR OF WALDECK-PYRMONT

Georg Viktor   —married—   Helene of Nassau
1831-1893   1831-1888

Sophie 1854-1869		*Died aged 15 of tuberculosis, or perhaps pneumonia*
Pauline —married— 1855-1925	Alexis of Bentheim & Steinfurt	*Pauline was originally the subject of King Willem III's attentions, but stood aside for her sister Emma*
Marie —married— 1857-1882	Wilhelm Crown Prince of Württemberg 1848-1921 *later King Wilhelm II of Württemberg*	*Marie died in childbirth, aged 24, with her third child (a stillborn daughter)*
Emma —married— 1858-1934	King Willem III of the Netherlands 1817-1890	*Emma and the king had one child, who succeeded her father as Queen Wilhelmina*
Helene —married— 1861-1922	Leopold Duke of Albany 1853-1884 *Son of Queen Victoria*	*Leopold died from haemophilia following a fall, after two years of marriage. His posthumous son,Karl Eduard, became Duke of Saxe-Coburg-Gotha*
Friedrich —married— 1865-1946	Bathildis of Schaumburg-Lippe	*The only son of Georg Viktor, was the last reigning Prince of Waldeck-Pyrmont*
Elisabeth —married— 1873-1961	Alexander of Erbach-Schönberg	

4. THE MARRIAGES & CHILDREN OF
KING WILLEM III OF THE NETHERLANDS

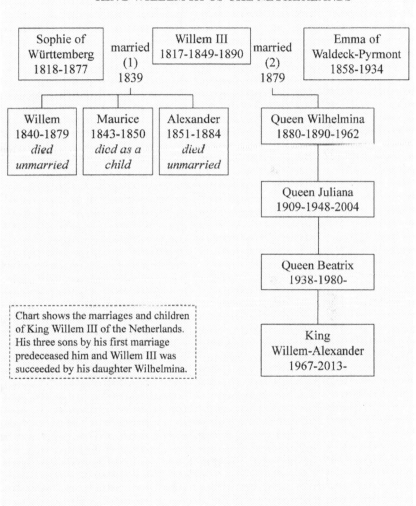

Sophie of Württemberg 1818-1877	married (1) 1839	Willem III 1817-1849-1890	married (2) 1879	Emma of Waldeck-Pyrmont 1858-1934

Willem 1840-1879 *died unmarried*	Maurice 1843-1850 *died as a child*	Alexander 1851-1884 *died unmarried*	Queen Wilhelmina 1880-1890-1962

Queen Juliana
1909-1948-2004

Queen Beatrix
1938-1980-

Chart shows the marriages and children of King Willem III of the Netherlands. His three sons by his first marriage predeceased him and Willem III was succeeded by his daughter Wilhelmina.

King
Willem-Alexander
1967-2013-

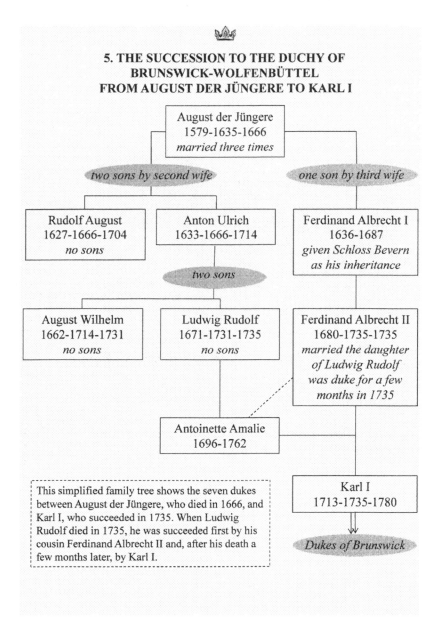

**5. THE SUCCESSION TO THE DUCHY OF
BRUNSWICK-WOLFENBÜTTEL
FROM AUGUST DER JÜNGERE TO KARL I**

August der Jüngere
1579-1635-1666
married three times

two sons by second wife

one son by third wife

Rudolf August
1627-1666-1704
no sons

Anton Ulrich
1633-1666-1714

Ferdinand Albrecht I
1636-1687
*given Schloss Bevern
as his inheritance*

two sons

August Wilhelm
1662-1714-1731
no sons

Ludwig Rudolf
1671-1731-1735
no sons

Ferdinand Albrecht II
1680-1735-1735
*married the daughter
of Ludwig Rudolf
was duke for a few
months in 1735*

Antoinette Amalie
1696-1762

This simplified family tree shows the seven dukes
between August der Jüngere, who died in 1666, and
Karl I, who succeeded in 1735. When Ludwig
Rudolf died in 1735, he was succeeded first by his
cousin Ferdinand Albrecht II and, after his death a
few months later, by Karl I.

Karl I
1713-1735-1780

Dukes of Brunswick

6. A SIMPLIFIED HISTORY OF THE ANHALT PRINCIPALITIES

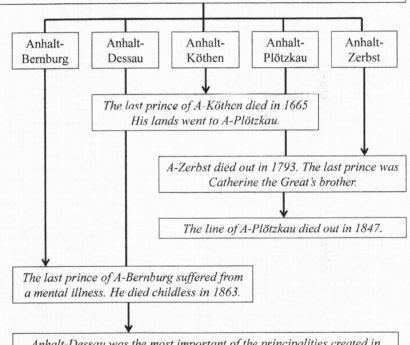

> Joachim Ernst, prince of Anhalt, 1536-1586
> *After his death there was a major dispute between his sons. In 1603 Anhalt was divided into four principalities, with Anhalt-Plötzkau added in 1611.*

| Anhalt-Bernburg | Anhalt-Dessau | Anhalt-Köthen | Anhalt-Plötzkau | Anhalt-Zerbst |

> *The last prince of A-Köthen died in 1665*
> *His lands went to A-Plötzkau.*

> *A-Zerbst died out in 1793. The last prince was Catherine the Great's brother.*

> *The line of A-Plötzkau died out in 1847.*

> *The last prince of A-Bernburg suffered from a mental illness. He died childless in 1863.*

> *Anhalt-Dessau was the most important of the principalities created in 1603 and went to the eldest son. After A-Bernburg was extiguished, it became the duchy of Anhalt.*

7. FAMILY TREE FOR THE PRINCES OF ANHALT-DESSAU FROM "DER ALTE DESSAUER" TO "VATER FRANZ"

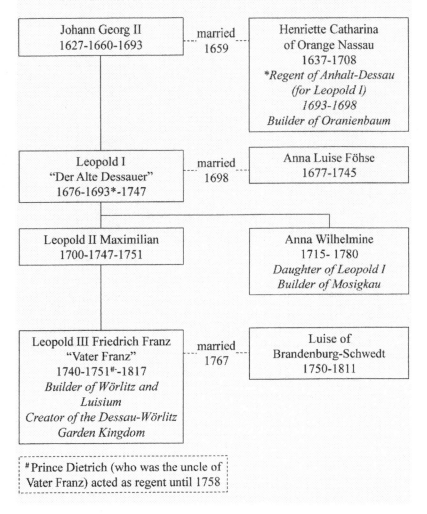

Johann Georg II
1627-1660-1693

married
1659

Henriette Catharina
of Orange Nassau
1637-1708
*Regent of Anhalt-Dessau
(for Leopold I)
1693-1698
Builder of Oranienbaum*

Leopold I
"Der Alte Dessauer"
1676-1693*-1747

married
1698

Anna Luise Föhse
1677-1745

Leopold II Maximilian
1700-1747-1751

Anna Wilhelmine
1715- 1780
*Daughter of Leopold I
Builder of Mosigkau*

Leopold III Friedrich Franz
"Vater Franz"
1740-1751#-1817
*Builder of Wörlitz and
Luisium
Creator of the Dessau-Wörlitz
Garden Kingdom*

married
1767

Luise of
Brandenburg-Schwedt
1750-1811

Prince Dietrich (who was the uncle of
Vater Franz) acted as regent until 1758

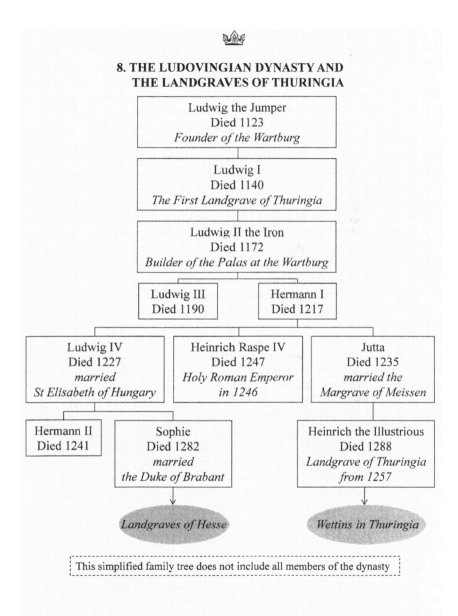

8. THE LUDOVINGIAN DYNASTY AND THE LANDGRAVES OF THURINGIA

Ludwig the Jumper
Died 1123
Founder of the Wartburg

Ludwig I
Died 1140
The First Landgrave of Thuringia

Ludwig II the Iron
Died 1172
Builder of the Palas at the Wartburg

Ludwig III
Died 1190

Hermann I
Died 1217

Ludwig IV
Died 1227
married
St Elisabeth of Hungary

Heinrich Raspe IV
Died 1247
Holy Roman Emperor
in 1246

Jutta
Died 1235
married the
Margrave of Meissen

Hermann II
Died 1241

Sophie
Died 1282
married
the Duke of Brabant

Heinrich the Illustrious
Died 1288
Landgrave of Thuringia
from 1257

Landgraves of Hesse

Wettins in Thuringia

This simplified family tree does not include all members of the dynasty

9. THE ELEVEN DUKES OF SAXE-MEININGEN

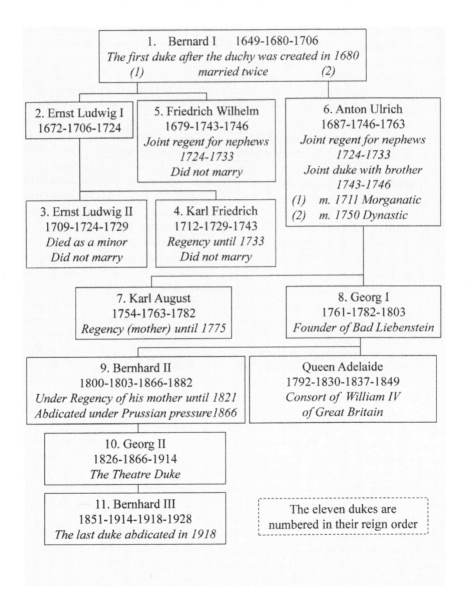

1. Bernard I   1649-1680-1706
The first duke after the duchy was created in 1680
(1)   married twice   (2)

2. Ernst Ludwig I
1672-1706-1724

5. Friedrich Wilhelm
1679-1743-1746
Joint regent for nephews
1724-1733
Did not marry

6. Anton Ulrich
1687-1746-1763
Joint regent for nephews
1724-1733
Joint duke with brother
1743-1746
(1)   m. 1711 Morganatic
(2)   m. 1750 Dynastic

3. Ernst Ludwig II
1709-1724-1729
Died as a minor
Did not marry

4. Karl Friedrich
1712-1729-1743
Regency until 1733
Did not marry

7. Karl August
1754-1763-1782
Regency (mother) until 1775

8. Georg I
1761-1782-1803
Founder of Bad Liebenstein

9. Bernhard II
1800-1803-1866-1882
Under Regency of his mother until 1821
Abdicated under Prussian pressure 1866

Queen Adelaide
1792-1830-1837-1849
Consort of William IV
of Great Britain

10. Georg II
1826-1866-1914
The Theatre Duke

11. Bernhard III
1851-1914-1918-1928
The last duke abdicated in 1918

The eleven dukes are
numbered in their reign order

10. THE RELATIONSHIP BETWEEN
THE HESSE-DARMSTADT AND BATTENBERG FAMILIES

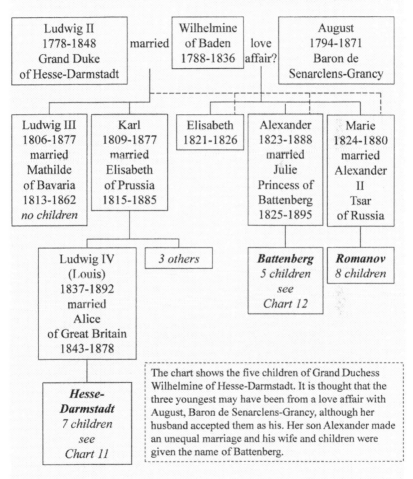

Ludwig II 1778-1848 Grand Duke of Hesse-Darmstadt	married	Wilhelmine of Baden 1788-1836	love affair?	August 1794-1871 Baron de Senarclens-Grancy

| Ludwig III 1806-1877 married Mathilde of Bavaria 1813-1862 *no children* | Karl 1809-1877 married Elisabeth of Prussia 1815-1885 | Elisabeth 1821-1826 | Alexander 1823-1888 married Julie Princess of Battenberg 1825-1895 | Marie 1824-1880 married Alexander II Tsar of Russia |

Ludwig IV (Louis) 1837-1892 married Alice of Great Britain 1843-1878	*3 others*	***Battenberg*** *5 children see Chart 12*	***Romanov*** *8 children*

Hesse-Darmstadt *7 children see Chart 11*

The chart shows the five children of Grand Duchess Wilhelmine of Hesse-Darmstadt. It is thought that the three youngest may have been from a love affair with August, Baron de Senarclens-Grancy, although her husband accepted them as his. Her son Alexander made an unequal marriage and his wife and children were given the name of Battenberg.

11. THE CHILDREN OF PRINCESS ALICE OF GREAT BRITAIN

Ludwig (Louis) IV —married—	Alice
of Hesse-Darmstadt	of Great Britain
1837-1892	1843-1878

Victoria —married— 1863-1950	Ludwig (Louis) of Battenberg 1854-1921 (later) 1ˢᵗ Marquess of Milford Haven *first cousin of her father*	*Two sons and two daughters – see chart 12. Victoria was the mother of Earl Mountbatten of Burma, and the grandmother of Prince Philip (husband of Queen Elizabeth II of Great Britain)*
Elisabeth —married— (Ella) 1864-1918	Sergey (Serge) of Russia 1857-1905 *son of Tsar Alexander II first cousin of her father*	*Serge assassinated 1905 Ella murdered 1918 by Bolsheviks No children*
Irene —married— 1866-1953	Heinrich of Prussia 1862-1929 *brother of Kaiser Wilhelm II first cousin*	*Irene was a carrier of haemophilia. Three sons, two of whom suffered from the disease*
Ernest Ludwig (Ernie) 1868-1937 —married—	(1) Victoria Melita of Saxe-Coburg-Gotha 1876-1936 *first Cousin* (2) Eleonore of Solms-Hohensolms-Lich 1871-1937	*Ernie's first marriage ended in divorce and their only child died aged eight.* *Two children from second marriage. Ernie's widow, son, daughter-in-law and two grandsons died in a plane crash*
Friedrich Wilhelm (Frittie) 1870-1873		*Frittie suffered from haemophilia and died after a fall, aged two*
Alix —married— 1872-1918	Tsar Nicholas II (Nicky) of Russia *second cousin*	*Alix was also a carrier and passed haemophilia to her only son. Alix, her husband and five children were assassinated in 1918 by Bolsheviks*
Marie (May) 1874-1878		*Died from diphtheria aged four, just before her mother*

12. FAMILY TREE FOR THE BATTENBERGS

Alexander of —— married —— Julie Countess von Hauke
Hesse-Darmstadt   1825-1895
1823-1888   Princess of Battenberg

Marie 1852-1923 m. Gustav of Erbach-Schönberg *4 children*	Alexander 1857-1893 Sovereign of Bulgaria 1879-1886 m. Johanna Loisinger *2 children*	Franz Josef 1861-1923 m. Anna of Montenegro *no children*

Ludwig (Louis) 1854-1921 Marquess of Milford Haven m. Victoria of Hesse-Darmstadt 1863-1950 *(daughter of Princess Alice)*	Heinrich (Henry) 1858-1896 m. Beatrice of Great Britain *(sister of Princess Alice)* 1857-1944 *4 children including Queen Ena of Spain*

Alice 1885-1969 m. Andreas of Greece & Denmark 1882-1944	Louise 1889-1965 m. Gustav VI Adolf King of Sweden 1882-1973 *no children*	George 1892-1938 Marquess of Milford Haven *married with 2 children*	Louis 1900-1979 Earl Mountbatten of Burma *Assassinated by the IRA married with 2 children*

4 daughters	Philip 1921- m. Elizabeth II of Great Britain 1926- *4 children*

13. THE LANDGRAVES OF HESSE-KASSEL AND THE BUILDERS OF WILHELMSHÖHE AND WILHELMSTHAL

> **Karl**
> 1654-1671-1730
> *Created the water garden and built the Octagon monument at Wilhemshöhe*

> **Friedrich I**
> 1676-1730-1751
> *Also King of Sweden from 1720*

> **Wilhelm VIII**
> 1682-1751-1760
> *From 1730 governor of Hesse-Kassel for his brother, the King of Sweden Built rococo Schloss Wilhelmsthal*

> **Friedrich II**
> 1720-1760-1785
> *Completed Wilhelmsthal Laid out Wilhelmshöher Allee*

> **Wilhelm IX**
> 1743-1785-1821
> From 1803 Elector Wilhelm I
> *Built Schloss Wilhelmshöhe in classical style and surrounded it with an English landscape park*

This chart shows the five landgraves of Hesse-Kassel
– from Karl to Wilhelm IX (elevated in 1803 to Elector Wilhelm I)

14. THE FOUR PRINCESSES OF ORANGE AND THEIR SCHLÖSSER

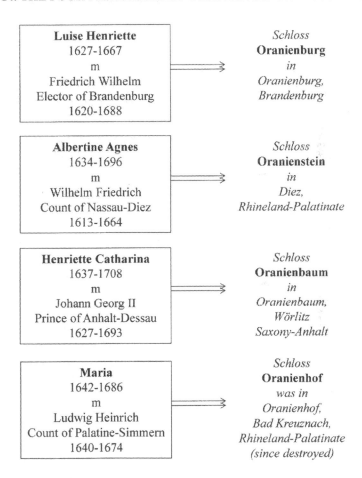

Luise Henriette 1627-1667 m Friedrich Wilhelm Elector of Brandenburg 1620-1688	*Schloss* **Oranienburg** *in* *Oranienburg,* *Brandenburg*
Albertine Agnes 1634-1696 m Wilhelm Friedrich Count of Nassau-Diez 1613-1664	*Schloss* **Oranienstein** *in* *Diez,* *Rhineland-Palatinate*
Henriette Catharina 1637-1708 m Johann Georg II Prince of Anhalt-Dessau 1627-1693	*Schloss* **Oranienbaum** *in* *Oranienbaum,* *Wörlitz* *Saxony-Anhalt*
Maria 1642-1686 m Ludwig Heinrich Count of Palatine-Simmern 1640-1674	*Schloss* **Oranienhof** *was in* *Oranienhof,* *Bad Kreuznach,* *Rhineland-Palatinate* *(since destroyed)*

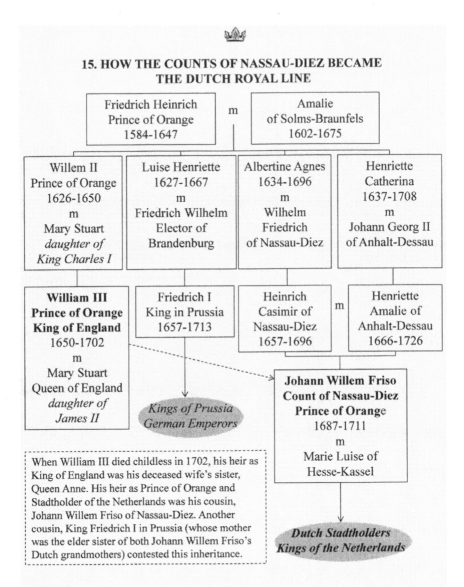

15. HOW THE COUNTS OF NASSAU-DIEZ BECAME THE DUTCH ROYAL LINE

Friedrich Heinrich
Prince of Orange
1584-1647

m

Amalie
of Solms-Braunfels
1602-1675

Willem II
Prince of Orange
1626-1650
m
Mary Stuart
*daughter of
King Charles I*

Luise Henriette
1627-1667
m
Friedrich Wilhelm
Elector of
Brandenburg

Albertine Agnes
1634-1696
m
Wilhelm
Friedrich
of Nassau-Diez

Henriette
Catherina
1637-1708
m
Johann Georg II
of Anhalt-Dessau

William III
Prince of Orange
King of England
1650-1702
m
Mary Stuart
Queen of England
*daughter of
James II*

Friedrich I
King in Prussia
1657-1713

Heinrich
Casimir of
Nassau-Diez
1657-1696

m

Henriette
Amalie of
Anhalt-Dessau
1666-1726

*Kings of Prussia
German Emperors*

Johann Willem Friso
Count of Nassau-Diez
Prince of Orange
1687-1711
m
Marie Luise of
Hesse-Kassel

When William III died childless in 1702, his heir as King of England was his deceased wife's sister, Queen Anne. His heir as Prince of Orange and Stadtholder of the Netherlands was his cousin, Johann Willem Friso of Nassau-Diez. Another cousin, King Friedrich I in Prussia (whose mother was the elder sister of both Johann Willem Friso's Dutch grandmothers) contested this inheritance.

*Dutch Stadtholders
Kings of the Netherlands*

Illustration Credits

Unless credited below, illustrations are from the author's collection.

2. Painting by Georges Desmarées, around 1746, © UNESCO-Welter-bestätte Schlösser Augustusburg and Falkenlust in Brühl. Photography Horst Gummersbach.
3. © UNESCO-Welterbestätte Schlösser Augustusburg and Falkenlust in Brühl. Photography Horst Gummersbach.
4. © UNESCO-Welterbestätte Schlösser Augustusburg and Falkenlust in Brühl. Photography Horst Gummersbach.
6. Schloss Nordkirchen/State of North Rhine-Westphalia.
7. Schloss Nordkirchen/State of North Rhine-Westphalia.
30. Copyright Kulturstiftung DessauWoerlitz, Picture library, photo: Heinz Fraessdorf 2015.
31. Copyright Kulturstiftung DessauWoerlitz, Picture library, photo: Heinz Fraessdorf 2015.
32. Copyright Kulturstiftung DessauWoerlitz, Picture library, photo: Heinz Fraessdorf 2015.
45. Duke Georg II with Helene von Heldburg, Eugenie Stoetzer, 1860, Pastel, Meininger Museen, VI 73.
46. Meininger Museen.
50. moreimages/Shutterstock.com.
52. Sixteenth-century portrait of Philipp of Hesse by Hans Brosamer, Everett-Art/Shutterstock.com.
73. Promenade before breakfast by George Barnard; lithograph of 1840 – Museum/Stadtarchiv Bad Ems.
75. Museum/Stadtarchiv Bad Ems.
78. Schloss Oranienstein/Museum Nassau-Oranien.
79. Schloss Oranienstein/Museum Nassau-Oranien.

Notes

Chapter 2

1. Denis Kretzschmar, 'State visits and flying visits to Schloss Augustusburg during the 19ᵗʰ century' in *A Republic Unrolls the Carpet: State Receptions in Schloss Augustusburg 1949-1996*, (Berlin and Munich: Deutscher Kunstverlag, 2008), 105-106.

2. Queen Victoria's journal, RA VIC/MAIN/QVJ (W) Monday 11 August 1845 (Princess Beatrice's copies), retrieved 28 October, 2015.

3. Holger Kempkens, 'Clemens August of Bavaria, Master of the House' in *Augustusburg Palace, Brühl*, (Berlin and Munich: Deutscher Kunstverlag, 2010), 4. During the War of the Spanish Succession (1701-14) Maxilimilian II Emmanuel allied himself with King Louis XIV of France, against the Holy Roman emperor. In 1704 he was exiled from Bavaria and his family was split up; they were not reunited until 1715.

4. Kempkens, *Augustusburg Palace, Brühl*, 6.

5. Kempkens, *Augustusburg Palace, Brühl*, 7-8. Clemens August had already been made bishop of Regensburg in Bavaria in 1716. When he got Paderborn and Münster he passed on this office to his youngest brother, Johann Theodore.

6. Marcus Binney and Alex Starkey, *Great Houses of Europe: From the Archives of Country Life*, (London: Aurum Press, 2003), 59.

7. Binney and Starkey, *Great Houses of Europe*, 59.

8. English audio guide at Schloss Augustusburg.

9. English audio guide at Jagdschloss Falkenlust.

10. Kempkens, *Augustusburg Palace, Brühl*, 10.

11. Kretzschmar, *A Republic Unrolls the Carpet*, 103.

12. www.schloss-tuernich.de

13. Conversation with Severin, Graf von und zu Hoensbroech.

14. www.schloss-tuernich.de

15. Kretzschmar, *A Republic Unrolls the Carpet*, 106.

16. Sara, Duchess of York and Benita Stoney, *Travels with Queen Victoria*, (London: Weidenfeld and Nicolson, 1993), 61.

17. Marcel Saché and Tony Crawford, *Nordkirchen Palace*, (Berlin and Munich: Deutscher Kunstverlag, 2011), 19.

18. Saché and Crawford, *Nordkirchen Palace*, 24.

19. *The History of Nordkirchen*, (a short leaflet available from the information office at Nordkirchen) suggested a much higher value of Euros 40-55 million, which is an exchange rate of one thaler to one hundred and sixty euros (taking the lower end of the range). However, this conflicts with a

much lower value suggested by another schloss, also for the eighteenth century, of one thaler to sixty euros (see note 27 in chapter four). It is impossible to value this old German currency accurately, but my research suggests that, when estimating, it is prudent to use the lower value.

20. Baron Pöllnitz, quoted in Saché and Crawford, *Nordkirchen Palace*, 25.
21. English audio guide at Jagdschloss Falkenlust.
22. Kempkens, *Augustusburg Palace, Brühl*, 9.
23. Binney and Starkey, *Great Houses of Europe*, 56.
24. Saché and Crawford, *Nordkirchen Palace*, 26-28.
25. *Althoff Grandhotel Schloss Bensberg, Bergisch Gladbach*, one-page handout about its history, available at the hotel.
26. Christopher Hibbert, *The Rise and Fall of the House of Medici*, (Newton Abbott: Readers Union, 1975), 310 311.
27. Helen Roche, *Sparta's German Children: The Ideal of Ancient Sparta in the Royal Prussian Cadet-Corps, 1818-1920, and in National Socialist Elite Schools (The Napolas), 1933-1945*, (Classical Press of Wales, 2013), 6.
28. Roche, *Sparta's German Children*, 199, note 33, from Heinich A, 'Niemand entgeht seiner Zeit', *Erziehung, Lernen und Leben in der Nationalpolitischen Erziehungsanstalt (Napola) Bensberg bei Köln: September 1942 bis April 1945*. Norderstedt. The ditty is from Bensberg's time as a Napola.
29. Roche, *Sparta's German Children* has an illustration of the practice of bacon swallowing on page 58, and of the Spanish rack on pages 62 and 84.
30. Roche, *Sparta's German Children*, 181.
31. Luise-Sophie, Princess Friedrich Leopold of Prussia, *Behind the Scenes at The Prussian Court*, (London: John Murray, 1939), chapter 11, 166-177.
32. Kries Coesfeld, *Burg Vischering: Lüdinghausen*, leaflet in English.
33. Joachim Zeune, *Castles and Palaces: Germany*, (Regensburg: Schmidt Verlag, 2004), 47.
34. Kries Coesfeld, *Burg Vischering*.
35. Christopher Clark, *Iron Kingdom: The Rise and Downfall of Prussia 1600–1947*, (London: Penguin Books, 2007), 10.
36. Stephan Sensen, *Altena Castle: Knights, Blacksmiths, Wayfarers – Short Guide Through the Permanent Museums*, (Altena: Märkischer Kreis, 2005), 21.
37. Sensen, *Altena Castle*, 31.
38. Sensen, *Altena Castle*, 35.
39. Gerhard Peters, *Fürstliches Residenzschloss Detmold*, (Detmold: Topp+ Möller, 2008) 7.
40. Peters, *Fürstliches Residenzschloss Detmold*, 8.
41. Ricardo Mateos Sáinz de Medrano, 'The Tiny Principality of Lippe.' *Royalty Digest: A Journal of Record*. November 1992, 145.

42. Empress Friedrich's letter to Crown Princess Sophie of Greece (her daughter), in Sáinz de Medrano, 'The Tiny Principality of Lippe', 145.
43. Empress Friedrich in the same letter to Crown Princess Sophie, quoted in Sáinz de Medrano, 'The Tiny Principality of Lippe', 145.
44. Sáinz de Medrano, 'The Tiny Principality of Lippe', 146.

Chapter 3
1. www.almanachdegotha.org , Principality of Waldeck-Pyrmont.
2. Torsten Haarmann, *Das Haus Waldeck und Pyrmont: Mehr als 900 Jahre Gesamtgesichte mit Stammfolg,* (Werl: Börde-Verlag, 2014), 40.
3. Haarmann, *Das Haus Waldeck und Pyrmont,* 42.
4. By 1882, when Helene married, haemophilia was a recognised disease and its hereditary nature was known. See Charlotte Zeepvat, *Prince Leopold,* (Stroud: Sutton Publishing, 1999), 14-16.
5. Arnout van Cruyningen, *The Dutch Royal Family: An Introduction to the House of Orange and the Monarchy in the Netherlands,* (mijnbestseller.nl, 2013), 35.
6. Roger Fulford (edited), *Dearest Child, Private correspondence of Queen Victoria and the Crown Princess of Prussia, 1858-1861.*London: Evans Brothers, 1964, 255. Quoted in Charlotte Zeepvat, 'A Minnow in the Shark Pool', *Royalty Digest: A Journal Of Record,* January 2003, (part 1), 195.
7. Zeepvat, 'A Minnow in the Shark Pool', 197.
8. Van Cruyningen, *The Dutch Royal Family,* 37.
9. 'The Times 21 March 1934' reprinted in *Royalty Digest: A Journal of Record,* August 2000, 46.
10. A. Stephan Jellinek and Anne Telp. *Nächtliches Schloss erleben: Heft Deutsch, English – Weserrenaissance Schloss Bevern.* Holzminden: Landkries Holzminden.
11. The book is *The Adventures of Baron Münchausen* by Rudolph Erich Raspe, first published in 1785.
12. Freundeskreis Schloss Bevern e.V. (edited), *Schloss Bevern: Als Fürstliche Residenz* (Holzminden: Freundeskreis Schloss Bevern e.V., 2013)11.
13. Jellinek and Telp, *Nächtliches Schloss erleben,* 39.
14. Jellinek and Telp, *Nächtliches Schloss erleben,* 41.

Chapter 4
1. 'Freheit', 22 May 1958, quoted in Thomas Weiss, Roland Krawulsky, and Margaret Will, *Welterbe Gartenreich Dessau-Wörlitz,* (Rostock: Hinstorff Verlag, 2010), 59.
2. Weiss, Krawulsky and Will, *Welterbe Gartenreich Dessau-Wörlitz,* 59.
3. 'Urban policy: How to shrink a city', *The Economist,* 30 May 2015.

4. A tontine is a financial scheme where as subscribers die the share of others is increased, until the last survivor gets the entire property. The Neapolitan banker, Lorenzo Tonti, initiated the first scheme around 1653. *The Oxford English Dictionary: Second Edition*, (Oxford, Clarendon Press, 1989).
5. Walter Henry Nelson, *The Soldier Kings: The House of Hohenzollern*, (London: J.M. Dent and sons, 1971), 70.
6. Nelson, *The Soldier Kings*, 68.
7. Nelson, *The Soldier Kings*, 181.
8. Correspondence with Kulturstiftung Dessau-Wörlitz; Leopold paid 92,000 thaler to the court of the emperor. It's impossible to be precise about today's values, but using one thaler to sixty euros (see note 19 in chapter two), the figure is about Euros 5.5 million.
9. *Dessau-Rosslau: Good Reasons to Come Here*, (Stadt Dessau-Rosslau), 19.
10. Correspondence with Kulturstiftung Dessau-Wörlitz.
11. *Guided Tour Through Mosigkau Castle*, Unofficial English text.
12. *Dessau-Rosslau: Good Reasons to Come Here*, 9.
13. Michael Stürmer, Ursula Bode, Thomas Weiss, Uwe Quilitzsch and Daniela Clare, *For the Friends of Nature and Art: The Garden Kingdom of Prince Franz of Anhalt-Dessau in Age of Enlightenment* (Ostfildern bei Stuttgart: Verlag Gerd Hatje, 1997), 76.
14. Stürmer, Bode, Weiss, Quilitzsch, and Clare, *For the Friends of Nature and Art*, 91.
15. Uwe Quilitzsch, *Die Wörlitzer Anlagen* (Wörlitz: Kettman-Verlag, 2000), English section of this multi-language guide book (it does not have page numbers).
16. Weiss, Krawulsky and Will, *Welterbe Gartenreich Dessau-Wörlitz*, 35.
17. Maria Kroll and Jason Lindsey, *The Country Life Book of Europe's Royal Families*, (London: Country Life Books, 1979), frontespiece.
18. *Guided tour through Wörlitz Country House*, (Kulturstiftung DessauWörlitz, 2000), English handout available at the schloss, 3.
19. *Quedlinburg Castle Museum*, (Quedlinburg: Schlossmuseum Quedlinburg, 2007), 3. The top of the plateau measures around 210 feet by 520 feet.
20. *Quedlinburg Castle Museum*, 9-10.
21. Monika Mai, *Die Ideale Frau* (Quedlinburg: Städtische Museen Quedlinburg), 11.
22. Mai, *Die Ideale Frau*, 25.
23. Mai, *Die Ideale Frau*, 8.
24. J. N. Duggan, *Sophia of Hannover: From Winter Princess to Heiress of Great Britain, 1630-1714*, (London: Peter Owen Publishers, 2010), 147.
25. Mai, *Die Ideale Frau*, 9.

26. Zeune, *Castles and Palaces*, 21.
27. *Friederike Caroline Juliane, Duchess of Anhalt-Bernburg (1811-1902)*, (Bernburg: DIZ-Anhalt), leaflet in English.
28. Duggan, *Sophia of Hannover*, 149.
29. Mai, *Die Ideale Frau*, 26, suggests an exchange rate of one thaler (valued in 1757) to sixty euros in 2005. Using this rate the value of the severance payment is Euros 3 million.
30. Mai, *Die Ideale Frau*, 12.

Chapter 5

1. Günter Schuchardt, *The Wartburg – World's Heritage* (Regensburg: Schnell & Steiner, 2006) 5.
2. The definition of World Heritage Site is from www.oxforddictionaries.com
3. Schuchardt, *The Wartburg*, 7.
4. *Memoirs of the House and Dominions of Hesse-Cassel: Giving an Account of the Origin and History of that Illustrious Family; their Estates, Dignities, Court, Revenues, Forces, Religion, Titles and Arms. The Whole Accompanied with Political Remarks. London: printed for T.Cooper [1740]* (Gale: ECCO (Eighteenth Century Collections Online Print Editions), 6.
5. Hans Pörnbacher, *St. Elizabeth of Hungary* (Regensburg: Schnell & Steiner, 2003), 8-12.
6. English handout for the German guided tour of the Wartburg.
7. Günter Schuchardt, *Martin Luther (1483-1546): Monk – Preacher – Reformer*, (Regensburg: Schnell & Steiner, 2006), 14.
8. Schuchardt, *The Wartburg*, 14. The collection is called the *Wartburg Sermon Postils* and contains sixteen sermons for Christmas.
9. Maren Goltz, *Meiningen – Muse's Court Between Weimar and Bayreuth: Bach, Bülow, Brahms, Wagner and Reger in Meiningen*, (Meiningen: Meininger Museen, 2011), 23.
10. Goltz, *Meiningen – Muse's Court Between Weimar and Bayreuth*, 16.
11. *Theatre Town Meiningen* (tourist information brochure), (Erfurt: Verein Städtetourismus in Thüringen E.V.), 6.
12. Ricardo Mateos Sáinz de Medrano, 'The Theatre Duke.' *Royalty Digest: A Journal of Record*, (August 1995), 35.
13. John van der Kiste, *Charlotte and Feodora: A Troubled Mother-Daughter Relationship in Imperial Germany*, (South Brent: A&F Publications, 2015), 14.
14. Roger Fulford (edited), *Darling Child: Private Correspondence of Queen Victoria and the German Crown Princess 1871-1878*, (London: Evans Brothers Ltd, 1976), 82.
15. Goltz, *Meiningen – Muse's Court Between Weimar and Bayreuth*, 7.

16. Mary Hopkirk, *Queen Adelaide* (London: John Murray, 1946), 44.
17. Hopkirk, *Queen Adelaide*, 141. This visit was in 1834 and the lady-in-waiting Lady Brownlow.
18. Dr. John Doran, *Memoir of Queen Adelaide: Consort of William IV (first published 1861)*, (Fairford: The Echo Library, 2011) 8.
19. Hopkirk, Queen Adelaide, 8.
20. Audio-guide at Schloss Elisabethenburg, Meiningen.
21. Hopkirk, Queen Adelaide, 208.
22. Hopkirk, Queen Adelaide, 62.
23. www.thueringerschloesser.de (English page).
24. *Memoirs of the House and Dominions of Hesse-Cassel*, 12.
25. Dieter Eckardt, Helmut-Eberhard Paulus, Willi Stubenvoll und Günther Thimm (edited), *Schloss Wilhelmsburg in Schmalkalden*, (Berlin and Munich: Deutscher Kunstverlag, 1999) 51.
26. Eckardt and others, *Schloss Wilhelmsburg in Schmalkalden* , 45. The writer was the nineteenth-century German art historian, Wilhelm Lübke.
27. www.museumwilhelmsburg.de
28. *Memoirs of the House and Dominions of Hesse-Cassel*, 16.

Chapter 6
1. Roger Fulford (edited), *Dearest Mama: Private Correspondence of Queen Victoria and the Crown Princess of Prussia, 1861-1864* (London: Evans Brothers, 1968), 85. Letter from Queen Victoria to the Crown Princess of 2 July 1862 (the day after Alice's wedding).
2. David Duff, *Hessian Tapestry* (London: Frederick Muller, 1967), 71. Also Helena, Princess of Great Britain and Ireland (edited), *Alice, Grand Duchess of Hesse, Princess of Great Britain and Ireland: Biographical Sketch and Letters, with Portraits* (London: John Murray, 1884) 330-331.
3. 1888 map of Darmstadt (MKL1888) from *Meyers Encyclopaedia*, fourth edition, included in the German Wikipedia entry for the Neues Palais, shows the location of the schlösser in the royal enclave in central Darmstadt.
4. *Das Darmstädter Schloss: Denkmäler in Darmstadt*, Wissenschaftsstadt Darmstadt.
5. Duff, *Hessian Tapestry*, 95.
6. Helena, Princess of Great Britain and Ireland, *Alice, Grand Duchess of Hesse*, 124-125.
7. Helena, Princess of Great Britain and Ireland, *Alice, Grand Duchess of Hesse*, 123-124.
8. Helena, Princess of Great Britain and Ireland, *Alice, Grand Duchess of Hesse*, 297-298.

9. Duff, *Hessian Tapestry*, 94-95, unpublished recollections of Lady Milford Haven (Princess Alice's eldest daughter).

10. Anja Spangenberg, *Little Darmstadt-ABC: English Edition* (Husum: Husum Druck – und Verlagsgesellschaft, 2010), 56.

11. Spangenberg, *Little Darmstadt-ABC*, 57.

12. Helena, Princess of Great Britain and Ireland, *Alice, Grand Duchess of Hesse*, 163, letter of 27 June 1863 from Princess Alice to Queen Victoria.

13. Queen Victoria's journal, RA VIC/MAIN/QVJ (W) Tuesday 8 September 1863 (Princess Beatrice's copies), retrieved 21 August, 2015.

14. Queen Victoria's journal, RA VIC/MAIN/QVJ (W) Tuesday 8 September 1863 (Princess Beatrice's copies), retrieved 21 August, 2015.

15. Helke Giambertone (translated by), *Jugenheim: The Heiligenberg and the House of Battenberg/Mountbatten* (Jugenheim: Verkehrs und Verschoenerungsverein Jugenheim a. d. Bergstrasse 1863 e. V, 2010), 25.

16. Giambertone, *Jugenheim*, 31.

17. Marie, Princess of Erbach-Schönberg, Princess of Battenberg, *Reminiscences* (London: George Allen and Unwin, 1925, reprinted by Royalty Digest 1996), entry for 14 June 1870, 133.

18. Eckhart G. Franz (edited), *Haus Hessen: Biografisches Lexicon* (Darmstadt: Hessische Historische Kommission, 2012), 341.

19. It was a temporary reprieve; the marriage of Napoleon and Josephine was dissolved in December 1809 and three months later Napoleon made a dynastic marriage to Marie Louise, the daughter of the Austrian emperor.

20. Franz, *Haus Hessen*, 341.

21. Storyboard in the Russian House museum at Heiligenberg.

22. Franz, *Haus Hessen*, 342.

23. Duff, *Hessian Tapestry*, 138.

24. Duff, *Hessian Tapestry*, 139-40.

25. Giambertone, *Jugenheim*, 26.

26. Giambertone, *Jugenheim*, 26.

27. Duff, *Hessian Tapestry*, 140.

28. Duff, *Hessian Tapestry*, 147, unpublished recollections of the first marquess of Milford Haven (the eldest son of Alexander and Julie).

29. Helena, Princess of Great Britain and Ireland, *Alice, Grand Duchess of Hesse*, 243, letter of 28 July 1870 from Princess Alice to Queen Victoria.

30. Rainer Zuch, *Burg Friedberg*, (Regensburg: Schnell & Steiner, 2011), 32.

31. Helen Rappaport, *Four Sisters: The Lost Lives of the Romanov Grand Duchesses*, (London: Macmillan, 2014), 141-142.

32. Marie, Princess of Erbach-Schönberg, *Reminiscences*, entry for 24 August 1868, 108-109.

33. Gisela Bungarten, Sabina Kôhler and Lena Weber (edited), *Wilhelmshöhe Park: Europe's Largest Hill Park* (Regensburg: Schnell and Steiner, 2014), 9.
34. Zeune, *Castles and Palaces*, 36.
35. Zeune, *Castles and Palaces*, 37.
36. Conversation with curator at Wilhelmshöhe.
37. *Memoirs of the House and Dominions of Hesse-Cassel*, 56, 49, 50, 51 (the page numbering in this old book is out of order).
38. Michael Imhof, *Kassel City Guide* (Petersberg: Michael Imhof Verlag, 2009), 26.
39. Brendan Simms, *Europe: The Struggle for Supremacy: 1453 to the Present*, (Basingstoke: Macmillan, 1998), 156. Source Michael Hochedlinger, 'Who's Afraid of the French Revolution? Austrian Foreign Policy and the European Crisis, 1787-1797', (*German History*, 21, 3, 2003), 310.
40. English handout at Schloss Wilhelmsthal.
41. Theo Aronson, *The Fall of the Third Napoleon* (London: Cassell, 1970), 206.
42. Museumslandschaft Hessen Kassel, *Paten für Putten: Retten Sie die Putten von Wilhelmsthal*, leaflet for restoration appeal.
43. Franz, *Haus Hessen*, 121-122.
44. English handout for the guided tour at Wilhelmsthal.
45. www.museum-kassel.de
46. English handout for the guided tour.

Chapter 7
1. Robert R. Taylor, *The Castles of the Rhine: Recreating the Middle Ages in Modern Germany* (Waterloo, Ontario: Wilfred Laurier University Press, 1999), figure 2 on page 26, courtesy of Loris Gasparotto, cartographer, Brock University.
2. Taylor, *The Castles of the Rhine*, 57. Goethe quote from Horst Johs Tümmers, *Rheinromantik: Romantik und Reisen am Rhein.* (Cologne: 1968), 14.
3. Hans-Jürgen Sarholz, *Spa Resort Seit Drei Jahrhunderten: Kurhaus Bad Ems* (Neuwied: Görres-Druckerei und Verlag, 2013), 10.
4. Sarholz, *Spa Resort Seit Drei Jahrhunderten,*19.
5. Sarholz, *Spa Resort Seit Drei Jahrhunderten*, 20-21.
6. Hopkirk. *Queen Adelaide*, 70.
7. Hans-Jürgen Sarholz, *Ems That Mir Wohl: Russische Gäste in Bad Ems – Das Zarenhaus* (Bad Ems: Verein Für Geschichte/Denkmal-und Landschaftspflege E.V. 2006), 22.
8. Sarholz, *Ems That Mir Wohl*, 19.
9. Sarholz, *Ems That Mir Wohl*, 28.
10. English information sheet from Schloss Oranienstein.

11. Michael Nash, 'A Prince and His Progeny' (*Royalty Digest: A Journal Of Record*, August 1999), 55.
12. *Memoirs of the House and Dominions of Hesse-Cassel*, 30.
13. Fred Storto, *Oranienstein: Barockschloss an der Lahn* (Koblenz: Görres-Verlag), 37.
14. Binney and Starkey, *Great Houses of Europe*, 88, quoting a description of the Rhine by Alexander Dumas pére.
15. Werner Bornheim gen. Schilling, *Stolzenfels Castle*, (Mainz: Landesamt für Denkmalpflege, Burgen, Schlösser, Altertümer, Rheinland-Pfalz, 2008) 7.
16. Taylor, *The Castles of the Rhine*, 32.
17. Schilling, *Stolzenfels Castle*, 8.
18. Taylor, *The Castles of the Rhine*, 128.
19. Taylor, *The Castles of the Rhine*, 118-9.
20. Taylor, *The Castles of the Rhine*, 224.
21. Correspondence with Franz-Josef Schmillen, Rhens.
22. Schilling, *Stolzenfels Castle*, 10.
23. *Queen Victoria's Journals*. RA VIC/MAIN/QVJ(W) Thursday 14 August 1845 (Queen Victoria's drafts), retrieved 28 September 2015, (written at Stolzenfels).
24. *Queen Victoria's Journals*. RA VIC/MAIN/QVJ(W) Thursday 14 August 1845 (Queen Victoria's drafts), retrieved 28 September 2015.
25. *Queen Victoria's Journals*. RA VIC/MAIN/QVJ(W) Friday 15 August 1845 (Queen Victoria's drafts), retrieved 28 September 2015.
26. Robert Dohme, *Burg Stolzenfels: Ein Führer aus dem Jahre 1850*, (Mainz: Landesamt für Denkmalpflege Rheinland-Pfalz, Verwaltung der staatlichen Schlösser, Burgen und Altertümer, 1986 reprint of original 1850 book), 128.
27. Dohme, *Burg Stolzenfels*, 130.
28. John Sherer, *Europe Illustrated: Its Picturesque Scenes and Places of Note*, (London: The London Printing and Publishing Company Ltd, late nineteenth century), volume 2, 145.
29. Conversation with curator at Stolzenfels.

Reflections
1. Sáinz de Medrano, 'The Tiny Principality of Lippe',146.
2. Arturo E. Beéche, *The Coburgs of Europe: The Rise and Fall of Queen Victoria and Prince Albert's European Family*, (East Richmond Heights: Eurohistory.com, 2014), 343-4.
3. Duchess of York and Stoney, *Travels with Queen Victoria*, 74.

Bibliography

Aronson, Theo. *The Fall of the Third Napoleon.* London: Cassell, 1970.

Barclay, David E. *Frederick Wilhelm IV and the Prussian Monarchy, 1840-1861.* Oxford: Clarendon Press, 1995.

Baumann, Arno. *Diez an der Lahn.* Verlag Der Rheinländer, 2011.

Binney, Marcus and Alex Starkey. *Great Houses of Europe: From the Archives of Country Life.* London: Aurum Press, 2003.

Brand, Ulrich (edited). *Bad Ems: A Short Introduction to its History and its Main Historical Buildings.* Bad Ems: Verein Für Geschichte/Denkmal – und Landschaftspflege E.V., 2002.

Broers, Michael. *Europe Under Napoleon.* London: I.B. Taurus, 2015.

Bungarten, Gisela, Sabina Köhler and Lena Weber (edited). *Wilhelmshöhe Park: Europe's Largest Hill Park.* Regensburg: Schnell and Steiner, 2014.

Clark, Christopher. *Iron Kingdom: The Rise and Downfall of Prussia 1600-1947.* London: Penguin Books, 2007.

Cruyningen, van Arnout. *The Dutch Royal Family: An Introduction to the House of Orange and the Monarchy in the Netherlands.*mijnbestseller.nl, 2013.

Discover Quedlinburg. Wernigerode: Schmidt-Buch-Verlag, 2014.

Dohme, Robert. *Burg Stolzenfels: Ein Führer aus dem Jahre 1850.* Mainz: Landesamt für Denkmalpflege Rheinland-Pfalz, Verwaltung der staatlichen Schlösser, Burgen und Altertümer, 1986 reprint of original 1850 book.

Doran, Dr. John. *Memoir of Queen Adelaide: Consort of William IV (first published 1861).* Fairford: The Echo Library, 2011.

Duff, David. *Hessian Tapestry.* London: Frederick Muller, 1967.

Duggan, J. N. *Sophia of Hannover: From Winter Princess to Heiress of Great Britain, 1630-1714.* London: Peter Owen Publishers, 2010.

Eckardt, Dieter, Helmut-Eberhard Paulus, Willi Stubenvoll und Günther Thimm (edited). *Schloss Wilhelmsburg in Schmalkalden.* Berlin and Munich: Deutscher Kunstverlag, 1999.

Franz, Eckhart G. (edited). *Haus Hessen: Biografisches Lexicon.* Darmstadt: Hessische Historische Kommission, 2012.

Freundeskreis Schloss Bevern e.V. (edited). *Schloss Bevern: Als Fürstliche Residenz.* Holzminden: Freundeskreis Schloss Bevern e.V., 2013.

Gehrlien, Thomas. *Das Haus Anhalt: Über 900 Jahre Gesamtgeschichte mit Stammfolgen.* Werl: Börde-Verlag, 2013.

Gehrlien, Thomas. *Das Haus Sachsen-Meiningen: Über 1000 Jahre Gesamtgeschichte mit Stammfolgen.* Werl: Börde-Verlag, 2013.

Giambertone, Helke (translated by). *Jugenheim: The Heiligenberg and the House of Battenberg/Mountbatten.* Jugenheim: Verkehrs und Verschoenerungsverein

Jugenheim a. d. Bergstrasse 1863 e. V, 2010.

Goltz, Maren. *Meiningen – Muse's Court Between Weimar and Bayreuth: Bach, Bülow, Brahms, Wagner and Reger in Meiningen*. Meiningen: Meininger Museen, 2011.

Haarmann, Torsten. *Das Haus Waldeck und Pyrmont: Mehr als 900 Jahre Gesamtgesichte mit Stammfolge*. Werl: Börde-Verlag, 2014.

Helena, Princess of Great Britain and Ireland (edited). *Alice, Grand Duchess of Hesse, Princess of Great Britain and Ireland: Biographical Sketch and Letters, with Portraits*. London: John Murray, 1884.

Hopkirk, Mary. *Queen Adelaide.* London: John Murray, 1946.

Imhof, Michael. *Kassel City Guide*. Petersberg: Michael Imhof Verlag, 2009.

Jellinek, A. Stephan and Anne Telp. *Nächtliches Schloss erleben: Heft Deutsch, English – Weserrenaissance Schloss Bevern*. Holzminden: Landkries Holzminden.

Kempkens, Holger, Marc Jumpers, and others. *Augustusburg Palace: Brühl*. Berlin and Munich: Deutscher Kunstverlag, 2010.

Kleine, Joseph. *Das Haus Lippe: Von den Ursprüngen bis zur Gegenwart*. Werl: Börde-Verlag, 2012.

Kretzschmar, Denis and others. *A Republic Unrolls the Carpet: State Receptions in Schloss Augustusburg 1949-1996*. Berlin and Munich: Deutscher Kunstverlag, 2008.

Lorenz, Dr Hermann. *Die Geschichte Anhalts in Wort und Bild: Für Schule und Haus*. Dessau: Anhalt Edition Dessau, 2007 (reprint der Ausgabe von 1906).

Louda, Jîrí and Michael Maclagan. *Lines of Succession: Heraldry of the Royal Families of Europe*. London: Orbis Publishing, 1981.

Mai, Monika *Die Ideale Frau*. Quedlinburg: Städtische Museen Quedlinburg.

Marie, Princess of Erbach-Schönberg, Princess of Battenberg. *Reminiscenses*. London: George Allen and Unwin, 1925, reprinted by Royalty Digest 1996.

Massie, Robert K. *Catherine The Great: Portrait of a Woman*. London: Head of Zeus Ltd, 2013.

Memoirs of the House and Dominions of Hesse-Cassel: Giving an Account of the Origin and History of that Illustrious Family; their Estates, Dignities, Court, Revenues, Forces, Religion, Titles and Arms. The Whole Accompanied with Political Remarks. London: printed for T.Cooper [1740]. Gale: ECCO (Eighteenth Century Collections Online Print Editions.

Merten, Klaus. *German Castles and Palaces*. London: Thames and Hudson, 1999.

Miller, Ilana D. *The Four Graces: Queen Victoria's Hessian Granddaughters*. East Richmond Heights: Kensington House Books, 2011.

Nash, Michael. 'A Prince and His Progeny'. *Royalty Digest: A Journal Of Record*, August 1999.

Nelson, Walter Henry. *The Soldier Kings: The House of Hohenzollern*. London:

J.M. Dent and sons, 1971.

Peters, Gerhard. *Fürstliches Residenzschloss Detmold.* Detmold: Topp+Möller, 2008.

Pörnbacher, Hans. *St. Elizabeth of Hungary.* Regensburg: Schnell & Steiner, 2003.

Quedlinburg Castle Museum. Quedlinburg: Schlossmuseum Quedlinburg, 2007.

Quilitzsch, Uwe. *Die Wörlitzer Anlagen.* Wörlitz: Kettman-Verlag, 2000.

Rappaport, Helen. *Four Sisters: The Lost Lives of the Romanov Grand Duchesses.* London: Macmillan, 2014.

Reepen, Iris. *Museum Jagdschloss Kranichstein.* Berlin and Munich: Deutscher Kunstverlag, 2002.

Roche, Helen. *Sparta's German Children: The Ideal of Ancient Sparta in the Royal Prussian Cadet Corps, 1818-1920, and in National Socialist Elite Schools (the Napolas), 1933-1945.* Swansea: The Classical Press of Wales, 2013.

Saché, Marcel and Tony Crawford. *Nordkirchen Palace.* Berlin and Munich: Deutscher Kunstverlag, 2011.

Sáinz de Medrano, Ricardo Mateos. 'The Theatre Duke.' *Royalty Digest: A Journal of Record.* August 1995.

Sáinz de Medrano, Ricardo Mateos. 'The Tiny Principality of Lippe.' *Royalty Digest: A Journal of Record.* November 1992.

Sáinz de Medrano, Ricardo Mateos. 'Lippe – A Family Album.' *Royalty Digest Quarterly.* 2, 2013.

Sarah, Duchess of York and Benita Stoney. *Travels with Queen Victoria.* London: Weidenfeld and Nicolson, 1993.

Sarholz, Hans-Jürgen. *Spa Resort Seit Drei Jahrhunderten: Kurhaus Bad Ems.* Neuwied: Görres-Druckerei und Verlag, 2013.

Sarholz, Hans-Jürgen. *Ems That Mir Wohl: Russische Gäste in Bad Ems – Das Zarenhaus.*Bad Ems: Verein Für Geschichte/Denkmal – und Landschaftspflege E.V., 2006.

Schencks Castles and Gardens: Historic Houses and Heritage Sights. Hamburg: Schenck Verlag, 2012.

Schilling, Werner Bornheim gen. *Stolzenfels Castle.* Mainz: Landesamt für Denkmalpflege, Burgen, Schlösser, Altertümer, Rheinland-Pfalz, 2008.

Schloss Mosigkau: im Dessau-Wörlitzer Gartenreich. Berlin and Munich: Deutscher Kunstverlag, 2012.

Schöber, Ulrike. *Castles and Palaces of Europe.* Lisse: Rebo International, 2006.

Schuchardt, Günter. *The Wartburg – World's Heritage.* Regensburg: Schnell & Steiner, 2006.

Schuchardt, Günter. *Martin Luther (1483-1546): Monk – Preacher – Reformer.* Regensburg: Schnell & Steiner, 2006.

Sensen, Stephan. *Altena Castle: Knights, Blacksmiths, Wayfarers – Short Guide Through the Permanent Museums*. Altena: Märkischer Kreis, 2005.

Sherer, John. *Europe Illustrated: Its Picturesque Scenes and Places of Note*. London: The London Printing and Publishing Company Ltd, late nineteenth century.

Simms, Brendan. *The Struggle for Mastery in Germany, 1779-1850*. London: Macmillan Press, 1998.

Spangenberg, Anja. *Little Darmstadt-ABC: English Edition*. Husum: Husum Druck – und Verlagsgesellschaft, 2010.

Steinberg, S.H. *A Short History of Germany*. London: Cambridge University Press, 1944.

Stürmer, Michael, Ursula Bode, Thomas Weiss, Uwe Quilitzsch and Daniela Clare. *For the Friends of Nature and Art: The Garden Kingdom of Prince Franz of Anhalt-Dessau in Age of Enlightenment*. Ostfildern bei Stuttgart: Verlag Gerd Hatje, 1997.

Taylor, Robert R. *The Castles of the Rhine: Recreating the Middle Ages in Modern Germany*. Waterloo, Ontario: Wilfred Laurier University Press, 1999.

Time to Travel: Travel in Time to Germany's Finest Stately Homes, Gardens, Castles, Abbeys and Roman Remains. Regensburg: Schnell and Steiner, 2010.

Timms, Elizabeth Jane. 'Kranichstein', *Royalty Digest Quarterly*, 2, 2015.

Victoria, Queen of Great Britain and Ireland. *Queen Victoria's Journals*. Windsor: The Royal Archives, 2012. www.queenvictoriasjournals.org.

Weiss, Thomas, Roland Krawulsky and Margaret Will. *Welterbe Gartenreich Dessau-Wörlitz*. Rostock: Hinstorff Verlag, 2010.

Zeepvat, Charlotte. 'Our Ardently Loved Hill', *Royalty Digest: A Journal of Record*, July 1995 (part 1) and August 1995 (part 2).

Zeepvat, Charlotte. 'A Minnow in the Shark Pool', *Royalty Digest: A Journal of Record*, January 2003 (part 1) and February 2003 (part 2).

Zeune, Joachim. *Castles and Palaces: Germany*. Regensburg: Schmidt Verlag, 2004.

Zuch, Rainer. *Burg Friedberg*. Regensburg: Schnell & Steiner, 2011.

THE SCHLOSS SERIES OF BOOKS

Schloss is the German word for castle or palace, and you are never far from one of these in Germany. For most of its history Germany was not a single country but a patchwork of royal states, held together under the banner of the Holy Roman Empire. The dukes and princes who ruled these states were passionate builders. Their beautiful castles and palaces, and their compelling personal stories, provide the material for the Schloss books.

This book can be seen as an inspiration ... to get out there and find the lesser known palaces and learn more about their history.
Royalty Digest Quarterly Journal.

Each of the Schloss books visits 25 beautiful castles and palaces in Germany and tells the colourful stories of the royal families that built and lived in them. Royalty have always been the celebrities of their day, and these stories from history can rival anything in modern-day television soap operas. The books are illustrated throughout and should appeal to anyone who likes history or sightseeing or is interested in people's personal stories.

Susan Symons has done another fantastic job, proving the point that history can also be fun...
The European Royal History Journal.

THE SCHLOSS SERIES OF BOOKS

The stories in the *Schloss* books include the mistress of the king who tried to blackmail him and was imprisoned for forty-nine years; the princess from a tiny German state who used her body and her brains to become the ruler of the vast Russian empire; the prince who defied his family to marry a pharmacist's daughter and then bought her the rank of royal princess; and the duke whose personal story is so colourful he has been called the Bavarian Henry VIII!

The latest addition visits Bavaria – and what a treat it is. Fascinating reading!
The European Royal History Journal

The German princes abdicated in 1918, at the end of World War I, and Germany became a republic. As they lost their royal families, many of the castles and palaces went into decline and became prisons, workhouses, and other institutions. Some were behind the Iron Curtain for fifty years. The books chart these difficult years and their resurgence and use today as public buildings, museums, and hotels.

The author's books are sympathetic to our fascinating royal history and make linkages and connections in a clear and interesting way.
European Castles Institute, Schloss Philippsburg, Germany

SCHLOSS WURZACH
A JERSEY CHILD INTERNED BY HITLER
– GLORIA'S STORY

Schloss Wurzach was a grand baroque palace built in the eighteenth century by one of Germany's noble families. But by World War II it had fallen on hard times and was used as a prison camp.

The schloss was cold, damp, in poor condition, and very dirty, when ten-year-old Gloria Weber arrived with her family and hundreds of other civilian internees deported from Jersey on the orders of Hitler. They were horrified by what they found. Twelve of the islanders died in Wurzach during their detention and are buried in the town; others suffered fractured lives.

This short book by Susan Symons recalls Gloria's childhood experience and is illustrated with vivid pictures of camp life painted by her father during their confinement. It also describes how she and other internees returned to Germany in later life to celebrate their liberation with the people of Wurzach, showing there can be reconciliation and friendship between former enemies.

ALL PUBLISHED BY ROSELAND BOOKS
www.susansymons.com

THE COLOURFUL PERSONAL LIFE OF QUEEN VICTORIA

Queen Victoria is the British monarch in history who's name everyone knows. These three books focus on the Queen as a woman – her personal life, events that formed her resolute character, and relationships that were important to her. They use some of her own words from her journal, to help tell the story; and are illustrated with portraits and memorabilia from the author's own collection.

Victoria has a life story full of drama, intrigue and surprises. *Young Victoria* covers the bizarre events of her birth, with a scramble to produce the heir to the throne; her lonely childhood under a tough regime; and how she came to the throne at 18.

Victoria & Albert is the story of her marriage to Albert and how she balanced the roles of monarch and Victorian wife and mother. *The Widowed Queen* covers the long years of her life alone after Albert's early death, when she became an icon of the age; the longest serving European sovereign; and matriarch of a huge clan.